CW00555699

ONCE UPON
A RHYME

Max Robertson

ONCE UPON A RHYME

Max Robertson

Foreword by
Sir Trevor McDonald OBE

Illustrations by
Loon

Prhyme Press

Text © Max Robertson 2000
Illustrations © Alasdair Hilleary 2000

Max Robertson has asserted his moral right under
the Copyright, Designs and Patent Act, 1988
to be identified as the author of this work

First published in Great Britain in 2000 by
Prhyme Press
c/o Lennard Associates Limited
Mackerye End, Harpenden
Hertfordshire AL5 5DR

A CIP catalogue record for this book
is available from the British Library

ISBN 1 85291 145 X

Cover designed by Paul Cooper

Printed and bound in Great Britain by
Hackman Printers

CONTENTS

STOIC AGE

IRONIC AGE

ACKNOWLEDGEMENTS

Adrian Stephenson, my publisher, has told me that he does not believe in what collectively might be called a 'fuss' of tributes, so I shall stick to his dictum.

Suffice then to say of the contributors that each knows their value to this project and my debt to them. I am indeed grateful to one and all. Besides Adrian there is Alasdair Hilleary (Loon), whose drawings (observations of life by a quirky eye) so enrich the text; Mark Adnit of Guernsey's Evolution Recording Studios, who has patiently followed my criss-cross trail through the minefield of virgo perfection; and my daughter Kate, who in a busy time of her own work and a demanding schedule of acting and writing for the Old Stagers, still remained faithfully on call for me as amenuensis and support. Pat Savill, too, has always played an understanding and helpfully critical role. Once more Buzzer Hadingham has been a literal-spotter of flycatcher sharpness and scanner of acuity. I am grateful to Roger Woods for his interest in the book and know that he and his staff will do their considerable best to persuade others to their view; and I want to express my deep debt to Paul and June Heald, my Guernsey friends, who have remained constant and imaginative in their total support

And now to Sir Trevor McDonald, who in a whirlwind of work – cyclone force during the celebrations of the Queen Mother's Centenary – climaxing at his departure on holiday, found an eye of mental energy to write a foreword for me. His support is tremendously heartening and gives me hope for my venture. I return him my heartfelt thanks.

Max Robertson
August 2000

P.S. A final thank-you to Michael Atherton, whose supreme performance at The Oval 'hey prestoed!' my 'supposing' of last March (Poem No 97) into such brilliant reality as a prelude to England's triumphant conclusion. **M.R. Sept 4th**

FOREWORD
by
Sir Trevor McDonald O B E

I am delighted to contribute a comment to this collection of poems by Max Robertson. I have come to the distinct view that poetry is as much a part of Robertson's life as it is of mine. His work bristles with a kind of infectious enthusiasm and one gets the impression that he writes with passion and with gusto. I admire the great range of subjects he covers, from the abstract like 'Disgust', 'Disquiet of Mind' and 'Destiny', to the more specific like 'Lorna de Lucchi', and, of course, the many tributes to friends and former colleagues like Brian Johnston, the great Fred Perry, John Arlott and Christine Truman. Max Robertson spent many years as a most distinguished broadcaster, working alongside legendary figures like Wynford Vaughan Thomas, who I was privileged to know and of whom Robertson says 'his Welsh gift for gusto and imagery never failed to bring a commentary alive'.

And therefore one of the fascinating things about this collection of poems is that they mirror Max Robertson's interesting life, as he played his part in the post-war expansion of the BBC, hosting quiz shows and children's programmes, doing travel shows and reporting on all manner of events before becoming, in my view, the voice of Wimbledon tennis on radio. My admiration of Robertson's work dates from that time, because I had tried to do the same in the West Indies before I came to England and had some idea of what a terribly difficult job it was. He made it sound easy and he brings the same marvellous descriptive brilliance to his poems.

Even with my great love of poetry, I cannot and must not pretend to be an accomplished critic. I have no idea whether Max Robertson's work will one day claim a place in the canons of English writing. They will however find a receptive audience for discerning readers keen to follow the progress of a great broadcasting career in verse. May we all be infected by Max Robertson's irrepressible energy and drive and by his golden memories.

PREFACE

Loon's drawing tells the story of this book, which owes more to my mentor, Ken Fletcher, seen here as the Buddhist god of longevity, Shou Lao, descending to his suppliant disciple, borne down by one of his familiars, the crane.

Ken Fletcher (late Senior and English master at Elizabeth College, Guernsey) by stimulating my interest; by gently guiding me in the principles of scansion; by praise of metaphor or raised-eyebrow disapproval of cliché; by using all the wiles of a good teacher, brought forth the small talent that was latent in me, and has given it enough polish to start my believing in myself.

He is always a ready reference, casting aside the *Times* crossword, which he normally does in about ten minutes; or letting his lunch cool while he considers my query. He can always find time, despite his many varied commitments, to give free help to the community.

In short Ken is an amazing man, who certainly helps me toward longevity by giving me purpose, stoking my will and desire to write verse.

This collection of my varia has come to press as an interim dividend. The final pay-out will be the sequel to a revised edition of *The Ballad of Worple Road*, to be called *Wimbledon – The Age of the Icons (1922-70)*, the two to be published together in time, I hope, for Wimbledon 2001.

The press in question is Prhyme Press. Why? Because I think modern poetry has gone too far in shaking off the so-called shackles of rhyme and rhythm. Lines of prose, however well written with splendid feeling and metaphor, should not, I believe, be regarded as poetry.

Let's get back to the old disciplines in the new millennium. Experiment with them, vary them, if you like, but stick to the principles and ride out their trammels. For me, the classic form is 'prhyme' – a rhyming poem. Modern poetry I think of as 'proems' or prose poems.

The orthodox Ken Fletcher I feel sure approves these ideals. He will again be a major influence when I try to complete the *Ballad* sequel. It will require great effort from me and I am confident Ken will do his best to keep the cog-wheels turning. He is an inspiration and support, for which I am truly grateful.

Max Robertson
August 2000

DEDICATION

This book is gratefully dedicated to all who appreciate the Queen's English, spoken or written, and in particular to John Snagge, whose deep and sonorous tones sounded the drum-beat voice of Britain that warned and warmed and rallied the nation – and the wider world – in the fateful days of World War II.

In peacetime, of course, the world remembers him best for his annual outing at the Boat Race, when he beat out the timing and rhythm of the oarsmen.

Away from work it was again a river beat that called to him; for he was a passionate fisherman.

His unique voice, with its hallmark of authority, always drew respect. He represented standards of English and enunciation imbued in the old BBC by a Scot, John Reith.

This tribute to a man of stature, who was always a good friend, was printed in the order of his Service of Thanksgiving at All Souls, Langham Place:

JOHN SNAGGE O B E

The Voice that tolled the nation's gravest hours
When Britain, girding fresh from late onslaught,
Was gathering force from springs of vigour fraught
By poisons burst from bombs of evil powers.

The Voice that timed the bowman's pendulum,
And gave a meaning count to all those strokes,
While bodies bent and stretched like ladder spokes,
Eyes fixed, ears harking cox as speculum.

For fifty years a man of great event;
For rest his zest of play with rod and line
In weathers hot or cold, careworn or fine,
His happiest hours in flirt with fish were spent.

Not one to brag but always fly the flag,
Our man at helm of History, John Snagge.

1 April 1996

Once Upon a Rhyme

INTRODUCTION

I was born in Dacca (now the capital of Bangladesh) on 28 August 1915. My father was the Engineer Burra Sahib (Chief Engineer) for the East Indian Railway, based in Calcutta. The engineering works were at Kanchrapara, 25 miles north of the big city. My sister Marian, a year and three-quarters younger, and I were looked after by an Indian ayah (nanny).

Like most families serving The Raj, ours was soon used to separation. We left India when I was five and a half and, after 18 months of pendulum living between boarding-houses, hotels, cousins, friends and grandparents (over 60 places in that short time), my sister was put in the care of a parson's family in Blandford. I, just seven, was left as a boarder at a pre-prep school in Winchester, run by a family that had been in India, in particular for boys in my situation. My mother became an anachronistic yo-yo between us and my father, who only had a long leave to come home every four years.

Like many sons of this situation, after four prep schools I went to Haileybury College near Hertford. 'College' because it was founded in 1826 as the East India College, the establishment that would develop boys into the young men who went forth to become rulers in India and the East. Being studious and sensitive, I had suffered some bullying at one prep school and would probably have sunk without trace at College (then known for its toughness), had I not been a good all-rounder at games.

For my last two years I had a study to myself in 'New Studies' on a wing of the lowest floor of a three-storey block, the three being long dormitories, housing some 50 boys each. The block overlooked 'Pavilion', the First XI cricket ground.

There were six similar dormitories on two sides of 'Quad', 110 yards square and the largest in England. These nine dormitories were dignified with the name of 'Houses', my own being 'In-quad' and called Edmonstone, after some Victorian worthy. The nine together were known as 'In-College' and we all looked down on the two 'Out of College' houses, Hailey and Highfield, which were proper buildings. Highfield particularly was stigmatised, because the fees there were higher and the boys were regarded as having a much softer time.

My study was a refuge in which I could dream and begin writing verse. I was reading a lot of poetry and my hero was Rupert Brooke. I knew 'Grantchester', 'The Soldier' and many others of his poems by heart. Fortunately my English master sometimes allowed me to experiment with my beginner's efforts, instead of suffering the grind of contriving a reasonable essay. I only got alpha minus from him once and that was not for a poem!

My 'single' study was narrow but had a view over a short lawn to the perimeter road that encircled the main College buildings, beyond which was 'Pavilion'. Every day, moving left to right, rather like a circus shooting-range target, I would see a College servant, the man whose job it was to gather up litter from the road and lawns. The boys' name for this 'familiar' was Offal-Bin Joe:

1. OFFAL-BIN JOE

Up the road he shambles
As, on wheels, he trundles
A dust-bin that rundles.

He's always labouring
(Meagre distended neck),
Always looks despairing
(Just a physical wreck),
His dreary sightless eyes
Fixed and staring ahead
In weird unearthly wise,
As if he's from the dead.

As along he rambles
And the barrow rumbles
With its many grumbles.

November 1933
Haileybury

Beyond 'Pavilion', my view ranged onto 'Lower Wood', a larger ground, about 10 feet lower than 'Pavilion'. The horizon was bounded by the wood. The nearest half of Lower Wood was the 2nd XI's home ground. During the week on quarter days, Tuesdays and Thursdays (when there was only an hour's work at 5.30 before evening chapel), Lower Wood would be the scene of three or four games of cricket for the lower orders of skill. It was the stamping ground of many a young cricketing McEnroe:

2. LOOKING ONTO LOWER WOOD
(Autumn at Haileybury)

Just one wisp of white shows in the pure sky,
Floating along, aimlessly drifting;
Caught by a puff of breeze, now shifting
From side to side, now low, then lifting,
Eddying on and passing vision by.
Down below the line of trees stands high,
Unbending, magnificent and still.
Today no hostile wind with icy chill.

And there the fields where on golden days
Boys play cricket – so many shouting
As they dispute, decision-doubting,
Contending, authority flouting.
Now, deserted, in fallow rest they laze,
Regaining strength to quell the summer blaze:
Out there all Nature reigns serene –
So peaceful, quiet and commonplace, this scene.

October 1933

"YOU CAN'T BE SERIOUS!"

At 18 I was beginning to write poetry and one subject that caught my attention was the start of what we now know as 'ribbon development' – the sprawl of new urbanisation. These two verses I intended to follow up but never did. I thought of it as:

3. RIBBON ENVELOPMENT
The Traveller (musing)

'So now I pause, my staff in hand,
And sadly mark the weary land ...
There droops the cote, there sags the mill,
Whose one-time wanton sails are still,
And now point, grimly gaunt and bare,
Skeleton fingers to the air.

There lie the stones, there leans the church;
There, starkly lone, uprears a birch
There in the church's leaky tower
The ivy chokes with pitiless power,
And rots the rope of the tongueless bell
That nevermore will toll a knell.

All the night through, throughout the day
Stalks the starved form of drear decay ...
Oh, tell me spirits of the air,
'Why this dead ruin everywhere?'

March 1934
Haileybury

Why didn't I carry on with that? There was plenty of material. I think the real reason for this was not so much laziness of mind as that I had only just begun my tottering first steps in versifying; and had yet to acquire the stamina needed for thoughtful work. My next illustrates this quite clearly:

4. DISQUIET OF MIND

Poor fool! Here I sit, restless, just wondering
What on earth to do; the whole evening before me.
Of course there's work, but that will only bore me.
And so I waste my time groping and blundering
My foolish way through the dark attics of my mind,
Trying to penetrate abstraction and to find
In some nook or corner of intelligence,
Something definite, if only commonsense.

And what do I find? Nothing. All is empty there,
Except for clinging cobwebs and ghastly bats
Hanging like corpses and squeaking, scuttling rats
That turn my brain to chaos, so that I despair.

Come thou, inspiration, with all thy former zest,
Give me occupation and set my mind at rest.

November 1933
Haileybury

Peace and certainty of mind I was perhaps granted – for the moment anyway, leading to this expression of confidence. In my 85th year I'm not nearly so sure:

5. THE ISLANDS OF THE BLEST

In the remoteness of the sky,
Beyond living power to reach,
Those holy thrice-blest islands lie.
No human prow has touched their beach,
But only angel vessels ply
Between those islands, each to each.
Nor may we, till we come to die,
O'erbridge the intervening breach.

When to us poor wretched mortals
Death has opened wide his portals,
And we at last the way are shown
To joy and happiness unknown,
And when we climb the secret stair,
We think of what awaits us there,
In those dear islands of the Blest,
A blissful peace, content and rest!

January 1934

But in my youthful development, feelings see-sawed at the slightest tilt and now I had sunk to my lowest depths:

6. CHAOS

Thoughts, thoughts, passionate thoughts
Flood my brain with fire,
Chasing each other hither and thither
In one dark-flaming, continual slither,
Thoughts that never tire.

Lust, lust, crumbling lust
Burns my body in shame;
In its filthy, blind, consuming pleasure,
An unbridled force that knows no measure
And always tastes the same.

Love, love, fleeting love;
I thought I knew my mind.
But each fresh face attracts my wooing
And each in turn proves my undoing.
Oh, Love, you are so blind.

The summer holidays at the end of my last term at Haileybury we spent at Selsey in Sussex. My father was with us and it was a halcyon time between school and an awareness that 'Life' was looming. We were staying by the beach:

7. EVENING BY THE SEA

Last trail of sunset blazoned in the west,
Sad eyes that watch the sure approach of night,
Which slowly spreads its tentacles of might,
And dims the weary world to quiet rest.

The great sea-mother rocks in cradling arms
The sands that nestle in her swirling fold:
She cools the burning land with kisses cold,
And dulls its throbbing pain with soothing balms.

The noise of day gives way to sobbing sough
That murmurs low in ceaseless lullaby,
And heavy hearts, refreshed with soft-drawn sigh
Are moved to offer up their evening vow.

Pale memories stir out and curling creep
Along the vagrant lanes that lead to sleep.

Selsey
August 1934

At the end of that Selsey holiday, my father returned to India. Marian had already gone back to school but I had a day or two before going up to Clare College, Cambridge. So I was able to join my mother in seeing my father off on the boat-train at Victoria – Platform 2:

8. P & O SPECIAL

The paper boys crying
And passengers buying,
Last frantic farewelling,
More buying and selling ...

'Goodbye, dear. Take care of yourself.
Don't forget, my salaams to Relf.
And, of course, give the rest my love.
Good heavens! Where's my other glove?'

A last-minute scurry
And bustle and hurry!
Passengers scrumming
And doors now slamming,
The guard's whistle's shrilling,
The windows are filling,
The train starts spluttering.
Handkerchiefs fluttering ...

'Phew! I'm glad we didn't have to rush.
It looks like being an awful crush.
Have you got the – Don't shove, Sir, don't shove!
Quick dear! There! There, at your feet! My glove!'

The train jerks out puffing
And quickens to chuffing,
The wheels begin sliding …
Now they are gliding,
They're off amidst cheering
And waving and blaring …
Now faces are blurring
They're soon out of hearing;
Only hands are showing;
But whose? … There's no knowing.

27 September 1934

Clare freshmen in those days lived out in rooms. This was a mistake that has since been rectified. It encouraged the unsociable to become more reclusive – a tendency on my part that was not helped by the attitude expressed here:

9. DISGUST

Fellows herding together
In the fumes
Of another's rooms
Drinking,
And smoking,
Laughing,
Chaffing,
And poking
Fun, winking,
And again – drinking …
I wonder whether
They ever
Do any serious thinking?

Thinking! … Ye Gods!
They only smoke,
… and laugh,
And chaff,
… and joke,
Sinking
… their personalities
With flushed trivialities
Drinking …
Oh! The silly clods!
Mouthing vile jests coarsely,
And laughing whoresly

With fat, lewd cackles,
Of debauchery ... my hackles
Rise in flame! ... The sensual sods!
Though I would wish to be one
Of them, to understand
Laughter, fun,
And a real hearty,
Helluva party;
Bear a hand
In everything that's done ...
Yet I cannot help but shun.

'Wine, women and song'
Rings in my ears
The whole day long.
Why don't I LIVE? ...
But something's wrong.
Such LIFE's a sieve,
And Nature's far too strong.

27 October 1934

It was four days later that I wrote:

10. REFLECTION

I look into my eyes,
And they wonder.
What is the great surmise
Keeps us asunder?

And are they really pure
In thought and deed?
Have they been always sure
To their true creed?

31 October 1934

What a young prig!

I was saved again to some extent by sport. I was playing a lot of squash and should have made at least fifth string in the University side that year. I would almost certainly have got into the Rackets Pair with John Pawle, a Harrovian who after the war won the Amateur Championship three times running and then gave up. One Sunday morning, playing him in a practice game, I won 5–0 but have to admit that he was suffering a hangover! He was the most perfectly balanced player I have ever seen, not excluding Geoffrey Atkins, a later world champion. John Pawle's stroke technique, forehand and backhand, was a mirror of flawless execution.

As to work, I was reading English and was awed by the other 'men' in my set, who all seemed brilliant. One tall, handsome redhead in particular appeared a demi-god. His name was Tristram Beresford, eldest son of the well-known author of the day, J D Beresford. He was a brother-in-law to be, for several years later I married his sister, Elisabeth, the creator of the Wombles and many wonderful magic books for children.

I realised that, if I were to get even a 'reasonable second', I would have to work very hard – a prospect that did not please. I felt I wanted to write as a career and wishfully wondered if I wouldn't do better to get experience of 'real life' in the outside world, knowing also that it would save my father a considerable financial strain keeping me at Cambridge.

So it was that I persuaded him (with backing, I think, from my mother who was a natural pioneer) to let me join a small group of people led by old friends from Indian days who, as 'The New Guinea Gold Syndicate', were venturing to Papua to look for gold. So I 'came down' (jettisoning forever any chance of real sporting success) and left for Sydney at the end of March 1935. The other chance that I unknowingly lost was that of being recruited into the Cambridge spy ring then being formed. Although I thought myself an idealist, I don't think I would have fallen for that one.

Before that I was able to pay one visit to Haileybury and rejoin old friends:

11. ALMA MATER

Today we did the same old things
We used to do when we were kings
Together. Oh! How I did long
To stay with you, once more belong
To ev'ryday routine of school –
Where one does not feel such a fool:
Where there is work (not much of it),
And games galore (for greater profit!)
Important things, like school and house
(For laisser faire a little nous) –

To muddle through quite comfortably
While life goes on interminably,
From term to term, from hols to hols
Like lists of dates and protocols.
Oh, Life of school! Its endless chat,
Its wanderings from this to that,
Its gramophones and study teas
While all are lolling at their ease;
Its faggables and smells of cooking
And breaking rules when no-one's looking ...
Ah, Haileybury! Ah, Haileybury!
How can she hear my feeble cry,
When famous men throughout the years
Have lived and laughed and wept their tears,
Have died and shed their own life's blood
To prove that they were of her brood?

She has no need of my defence,
But this I say to those gone thence,
'Of all who've played on Twenty Acre
Cursed be they that would forsake her!!'

February 1935
Chelsea

So, with four others of the follow-up to the advance party, which had already arrived in Papua, I boarded the Orient Line SS Ormonde for what then was a romantic six-week voyage to Sydney.

She was the first 'all-tourist' ship. One literally had the run of her decks, the exclusion zone being the forrard dining lounge, if your passage was costing less than £85 (I think). I was sharing a berth over the screw for £38.

There were many moonlit nights on the boat deck. This was written before I'd found anyone to share them:

12. MOONLIT MEMORY

In the moonlit silences of night
Memory came to me.
Borne on the wavering wings of light,
Softly she sped to me;
With her sweetly caressing fingers
She left a cobweb trace;
And her lightest touch still lingers
Upon my burning face.

April 1935
On board SS Ormonde

Not always were the seas calm and romantic:

13. THE LURE OF THE FAR UNKNOWN

The wallowing ship comes heaving up,
The stars go sliding down.
Men open wide their eager arms
To the lure of the Far Unknown.

Is it in vain that lovers strain
To reach for the stars above?
Will it always end in endless pain,
This seeking after Love?

For when they find that they've been blind
And idealised ideals,
It's not the heart's dis-ease they mind,
But the pain the spirit feels.

Ah God! To feel the cherished ideals
Have crumbled into dust!
To know that one no longer kneels
At the feet of Love – but of Lust!

And worst of all is the bitter gall
Of lovers who've lost their faith;
Because they know they've lost their all
And there's nothing left but Death.

The billowing sea comes heaving up,
The ship goes sliding down;
The stars are smiling to themselves
Up there in the Far Unknown.

It wasn't long before I had got to know two girl friends; both were New Zealanders. One was considerably older and really a very good aunt to me; the other much nearer my age and a very nice companion. I don't think I ever got beyond a peck on the cheek. They both left at Melbourne to trans-ship for New Zealand.

By now I had become aware of Nancy Suttor, a Sydney girl who had been spending a year in England. Her home was with her parents in a flat on Darling Point Road, Sydney's most exclusive residential suburb. I had barely started a tentative courtship when we disembarked, she to Darling Point and I to stay by arrangement with contacts in Cremorne on the east side of the famous bridge.

There I was, languishing with not long to go before I continued on a Burns Philp coastal boat, the old Montoro, to Port Moresby. My feelings show in the following:

14. THE TELEPHONE HAS JUST BEEN RINGING

Comes a tram ...
Stops to disgorge some passengers,
Fills its belly once again ...
Sighs ... wheezes ... groans ... and shrieks
In rising crescendo ...
And labours on its way ...

I sit and listen,
Thought-fuddled and depressed.
The telephone has just been ringing,
But not for me;
Errand-boys whistling and singing,
But not to me.

Odd sounds filter through the silence ...
A cart creaking on its way ...
Footsteps busied on some purpose ...
But I have lost my way.
Then the hooting of a siren ...
The crying of a child ...
The far-off busy-city rumbling,
An undertone of growling menace ...

The telephone has just been ringing!
Yes really just for me!
And now of course my heart is singing,
For she still remembers me!

23 May 1935
Cremorne, Sydney

The Montoro laboured up the East Coast. She was one of the regular supply boats for Papua, then an Australian dependency, and for adjacent islands. Burns Philp – or BPs (Bloody Pirates as they were known) were the wholesale suppliers on whom everyone depended – traders, prospectors and all who lived on the coastal fringe. BPs would off-load our stores (if we were lucky) at Kukipi, 100 miles or so up the west coast from Port Moresby and at the mouth of the Lakekamu River, of which the Cassowary was a tributary. Thence a launch brought them up-river to Bulldog, a small aerodrome hacked out of the bush, as the rain jungle forest was called. It was the HQ of a big company prospecting for gold by dredging.

From there our own 'boys' would porter them for 10 miles to our camp. Often they had to cross streams that were in spate by felling a tree as a bridge. We, in our army-style boots, teetered dangerously when negotiating these improvised bridges. It always amazed me to see one of the 'boys', bearing a heavy load, stop in mid-bridge (no handrail) and lift one foot to remove a leech.

*It was while waiting at Moresby for our next onward stage that I wrote
this:*

15. LOVE'S IDEAL

Love is a thing that must not be sought;
Love comes of its own, as quiet as thought
To the pale brow of dawn; for love is fraught
With the innermost things that are not bought.

Love pulses with life like the morning sun
That dances in dew, commingled in one;
Love moves with the strength of rivers that run
Through evening shadows when day is done.

Love sets in a blaze of burning red-gold
That splinters the sky to fragments untold;
Love is a youth that will never grow old
And breathes a pure flame that cannot burn cold.

Love is the highest of heights upon earth,
So high, so rare – of true love there's a dearth.

13 June 1935
Hotel Papua, Port Moresby

Our gold venture was a disaster in business terms, fully described in my book, Stop Talking and Give the Score *(Kingswood Press, 1987). It was when alone, except for some of our Papuan indentured labour, prospecting the higher reaches of The Cassowary, on which we had based our main camp that, resting at sundown, I became especially contemplative:*

16. ET TU?

Have you ever known
The pain of petal strown
From pride of rose?

Have you ever heard
The thrilling of a bird
In full-throat song?

Have you ever seen
The gentle, fading sheen
Of twilit sky?

Have you ever smelt
Sweet lavender or felt
A stirring breeze?

Happy he that knows,
Who has lived among
Such things. Happy I
To have known all these.

28 November 1935
Upper Cassowary, Papua

My feelings were probably triggered by the arrival of some mail, which often took weeks to reach us but was vital to sustaining morale. So stimulated, next day I was reminded of Papua's great catchword, 'Dohori', meaning 'Wait a while', as you might say to a messenger. It was known as 'The Land of Dohori', because nothing came quickly and, in the jungle, the 'Wait a While' thorn brought you to a standstill if you once became enmeshed:

17. WAIT A WHILE

Somewhere came a frog's croak.
Another took the cry
And filled the air with sound.
While darkness swept her cloak
Across the evening sky
And shadowed all the ground.

It was the hour of rest,
When, sitting in my chair
Quite still and calmly quiet,
I watched day fading west
And gave forbearing ear
To the froggish riot.

And then I thought of you,
Of your clear, level gaze;
Your hair; your secret smile ...
I wondered if you too
Did dream of happy days,
If we would wait a while.

29 November 1935
Upper Cassowary, Papua

The following two evenings were spent thinking of my godmother,
Lorna de Lucchi (née Lancaster), who had married an Italian count
and lived in Padua. She had been a schoolfriend of my mother and
was a poetess, whose translation of The Minor Poems of Dante *was*
the standard work. My mother had submitted some of my early efforts
to her and – I think unwisely – passed on her comment that she did not
think I'd got 'it'. I believe it had a fairly profound effect:

18. TO LORNA DE LUCCHI

When I heard a sweet voice singing,
Singing so softly sad,
Oh it set my heart a-wringing
Though I was but a lad.

So I looked and I saw her singing,
A pretty bird in a cage.
And her little feet were clinging ...
It set my heart a-rage.

I came to her and said, 'Sweet bird,
What is it can be wrong?
You sing as sweet as e'er I heard,
But why so sad a song?'

'Alas, fair youth, you cannot know
What t'is to prisoned be.
You, who today so proudly go
So happy and so free.

'I too was free long years e'er now
And sang full joyously;
Until I gave my love my vow,
My love from over sea.

'So strong he was, so kind, so good
That he quite conquered me.
To follow him I said I would
Desert my own country.

'And I, 'gainst call of kith and kin
Went with him over sea.
To have said no would have been sin,
I think you will agree.

'But though I love my lover still,
Love him devotedly;
Yet love of man's not all to fill
The gap of liberty.

' 'Tis true I have a gilded cage
And servants more than three,
Yet I would rather earn my wage
And have my liberty.

'And here I find it hard to sing,
Where all's discordant sound;
For the mad Deuce is marshalling
His men from all around.

'And he is teaching them to hate
My own, my kith and kin.
He tells them that they must not wait
But go right in and win.

'Ah! Then I know my heart's desire
With mine own folk to be;
To help them fight the madman's ire
And keep their liberty.

'Could I but see the land I love,
England my own country!
The land where I am free to move
And sing in ecstasy.

'So now you know why I am sad
And sing so bitterly.
I can ne'er again be glad
Until I am set free.'

Then sorrowfully I turned away,
Away from her sad song;
And I went wond'ring on my way
Had she been right or wrong?

Upper Cassowary
29-30 November 1935

After an ungilded year in Papua, back in Sydney, I managed to get a series of talks, 'A Pommy in Papua' on the ABC (The Australian Broadcasting Commission) and was encouraged to apply for a job as an announcer. Auditions went well but that seemed to be as far as I was getting. Whilst waiting anxiously, I kept my verse-hand in by doing several translations from the Oxford Books of French and German Verse. This is from a very sad poem by Ludwig Uhland:

19. THE INNKEEPER'S DAUGHTER

Three lads went riding far over the Rhine,
Till they turned in at an innkeeper's sign:
'Mine hostess, have you good beer and wine?
Where are you hiding your daughter divine?'

'My beer and wine are fresh and clear,
My daughter lies on her funeral bier.'
And when to the room they made their way,
In a black coffin there she lay.

The first that drew back the veil on her sleep
Looked at her sadly, as if he would weep:
'Ah! If you lived still,' in sorrow he said,
'I'd love you henceforward, beautiful maid!'

The second put back the veil in its place
And turned him away with tears on his face:
'Ah, that you lie on your funeral bier
When I have loved you so many a year!'

But the third once again drew back the veil
And tenderly kissed the mouth so pale:
'I've loved you always, I love you today
And I will love you for ever and aye!'

May 1936
Sydney

All this time I was continuing my courtship of Nancy. My love temperature was running very high when I poured out the five that follow, all written in October '36, whilst I had a temporary job teaching at Lochiel Junior Grammar School, Killara on Sydney's North Shore Line: from this strong emotion these resulted. The first two were born on the same day:

20. WE'D LET LOVE HAVE ITS DAY

I went into your room just now,
Sat down and looked about;
And I wondered 'Why?' and 'How?'
And tried to sort things out.

Oh, this eternal question 'Why
Can't we do as we feel?'
We love, we two, we love – then why
Can't we give love its seal?

My God, it's more than I can bear
To see you every day,
To have you ever-present, near
And yet keep love at bay!

I want you, you, essential you,
Your body, spirit, mind;
To do the things that we would do
If we were one in kind.

I want you now; I want to take
Your face between my hands,
And on your lips my love I'd slake
And kiss away love's bands.

And kiss and kiss until I'd chase
Those foolish doubts away –
And then in one long mad embrace
We'd let love have its day!

We'd cling and cling and feel the thrill
Of love that answers love,
At last, at last our love fulfil –
And then we'd never move.

No never move – but always stay
Close-clinging, face to face ...
To hell with what the world would say,
To love is no disgrace!

Killara
2 October 1936

No, but women are practical. Hence:

21. TO ONE WHO INSISTED ON HAVING A PROPOSAL IN WRITING

With the very humblest reverence I ask,
'My belovèd, will you be my wife?
Will you undertake the very thankless task
Of pacing me in the race of life?

Will you hitch your shining pole to my pale star
And join me for better or for worse?
Shall we drive off from the first and lower par,
Laughing at the hazards in our course?

Will you come with me to drink at the fountain
Of love thrilling with the joy of life?
Hand in hand shall we climb every mountain?
Oh, my darling, say you'll be my wife.'

2 October 1936
Killara, Sydney

And next a more intimate proposal:

22. SWEETHEART, SWEETHEART, LOVE ME TOO

Sweetheart, sweetheart, love me too,
And together we will do
So many things,
Oh, any things!
Things of love, love that sings
In ecstasy, love that brings
Perfect living –
That is giving
Of ourselves to one another,
Lover clasped in arms of lover!

11 October 1936
Killara, Sydney

By now the lover was in full throat:

23. SONG

Light of my life, my sweet, my sweet,
Give me your lips, your lips to greet;
Give me that look, that love-you smile,
That look that makes everything so worthwhile!
That look so sweet, that smile so fleet,
Give it me now, oh give it me now,
My love, my love, for here I vow
To love you for ever,
For ever, yes ever,
To love with a love that nothing may sever;
And never to fail you, never, oh never!
But love you always, love you above
Anything else in life, with a love
That is full, that is quick, that is tender;
With the love of my strength –
The love of surrender –
Till at length, oh at length,
Light of my life, my sweet, my sweet,
You give me your lips for mine to greet!

11 October 1936
Lochiel, Killara, Sydney

My wish was granted but I longed for more:

24. IT'S HEAVEN TO HOLD YOU
IN MY ARMS AGAIN

It's heaven to hold you in my arms again
My heart's treasure;
To listen to love's whisperings in my brain
Is sweet pleasure.

Your hair trails lingeringly across your face,
Passive you lie.
There comes a fleeting smile that leaves no trace
But my heart's sigh.

Infinite wisdom lies behind your eyes
And quiet brow,
So full of knowledge of Life's mysteries –
Oh yes, you know.

You know the joy of love, you know the pain;
Your soothing hand
Calms the quickening tumult in my brain –
You understand.

25 October 1936
Killara, Sydney

Courting, often every evening from that distance, proved my devotion and eventually I succeeded in getting a job as an announcer-cum-commentator, first in Sydney, then in Brisbane, where Nancy and I married. Not long afterwards, we decided to return to England where war was clearly looming. On the way back we were able to stay in Padua with Lorna. 'The Mad Deuce', Il Duce, Benito Mussolini, was indeed 'marshalling his men'. He attacked Yugoslavia whilst we were in Italy.

Back in London I managed to join the BBC as one of the first team of announcers for the new European Service.

On his retirement from India, my father had started farming Cox's Orange Pippins at Great Totham, near Maldon in Essex. He was very proud of the fine grandfather clock he had bought in a sale for £10 and installed in the hall. I always felt that 'Grandfather' understood:

25. GRANDFATHER RUMINATES

In a corner he stands
With benevolent face,
And round go his hands
At unvarying pace.

He's neither slow nor quick
Is the grandfather clock
With his questioning tick
And his answering tock.

For he's always just right
Is the grandfather clock,
And he knows he's quite 'quite',
Though upstarts may mock.

He's so self-assured
That, try hard though he does,
He can't help being bored
By all today's fuss.

'You really can't hurry me,'
His smile seems to say,
'So why do you worry me
In this ill-mannered way?

Nowadays, you know,
You all go too fast.
At the pace you all go
You can't hope to last.

For two centuries I've stood
And sounded my chimes,
Seen the bad and the good,
Watched the signs of the times;

And I never go fast;
I'm never too slow;
Through all the years past
I've gone on – just so.

But it's no good my saying
What I think of you all,
For you're none of you paying
Any heed to my call.

But one day you'll learn,
You'll get such a shock,
The truth you'll discern,'
Tocks the grandfather clock.

May 1939
Hill Home, Great Totham

Wartime saw me at first in a Territorial Anti-Aircraft Battery, the last formed before war was declared. So, on 1 September, after I did my final pre-war duty for the BBC, reading the Early Morning News on the BBC's Pacific Service, telling the world of Hitler's invasion of Poland, I made my way to Sevenoaks and joined the 83rd Light Anti-Aircraft Battery.

After a spell on gunsites in Kent and Essex and OCTU at Shrivenham (as cadet and then as an Assistant Adjutant), I was posted to the Maritime AA, newly formed as an army unit working to DEMS (Defensively Equipped Merchant Ships), a naval department hurriedly cobbled to cope with the war at sea.

An ex-Scots Guards corporal, now a wartime major, was running Maritime Ack Ack from HQ in Whitehall. Seeing my BBC and staff background, he summoned me to London from Portobello, where I was temporarily stationed. To get there and gain some practical experience, I took passage down the East Coast on a merchant ship, one of the Liberty ships (or vulgarly 'Sam Ships') welded hurriedly together from mass-produced sections in the United States on the Lend-Lease scheme:

26. A SHIP CALLED 'RICH'

They built a ship and they called her 'Rich',
Of the seed of Sam and a bastard bitch.
This cross-bred child has a dented screw;
When she goes astern she jars right through.

It matters not if she lasts five years
That she shakes like a shriek on startled ears:
It matters not if she lasts one trip
That she has the name of a happy ship.

Or so they thought – if they thought at all –
As they watched the champagne bottle fall.
Forgive that weak artistic licence.
Champagne! Good Lord, they had more sense.

But strange to say she's very rich
In the men who serve (they wouldn't switch)
As I can vouch who have made one trip
On 'Rich' (né 'Sam') – a happy ship.

1943

The major had hoicked me down to be the liaison officer for a film that was to be made on the Maritime Ack Ack in co-operation with DEMS. We set off in 1943 with a DEMS gun crew, selected not only for their functional ability but also, it was hoped, for their skills as budding film actors. (The proportion DEMS tried to keep was three Navy to two Army to underline their seniority.)

We were in a large Mediterranean convoy, each ship streaming balloons from its stern (we also had a 3.7-inch gun), expecting to run the U-boat gauntlet; but at that moment Italy surrendered and we saw her destroyer fleet carving through the waves between the convoy lines, as if in positive attack but actually bound for Tripoli, which the Allies had recently taken. The U-boat command was temporarily in confusion.

So our gallant crew was filmed doing the sights of the Pyramids and other Cairo spots. Whilst awaiting the signal for our onward passage to Sicily and Brindisi, I was billeted in the Palace Hotel, Port Said, where I had a very innocent wartime romance with a young French-Egyptian girl (no more than kisses by moonlight). Looking back later, I realised that she and her chaperone mother were almost certainly working for German or – more likely, British – Intelligence, checking on information that might be getting out to U-Boats about shipping coming through the Suez Canal:

27. MADEMOISELLE DIX-SEPT

Here in this palace we danced and talked,
Listened to music, then dined and walked.
Whatever we did, just you and I,
'Twas all the same to the moonlit sky,
When you were Mademoiselle Dix-Sept
And I was your faithful slave, Colette.

Was that only five short weeks ago?
A year? A day? I do not know.
Then life was sweet and love was a flower,
And my heart was prisoned in your power,
Oh lovely Mademoiselle Dix-Sept,
Remember the night when last we met?

The palace's rooms are empty now,
For Grace has gone, so has Beauty's brow;
And where we spent splendid nights and days
Is filled with dull, decrepit clays.
No music, Mademoiselle Dix-Sept,
Ah, would you were here, my sweet Colette!

The band is playing, the couples dance
Like random puppets controlled by chance.
(The Fates have woven my destined thread)
I cannot be one with them. Instead
My heart calls, Mademoiselle Dix-Sept,
Forget me not, for I love thee yet.

1943
The Palace Hotel, Port Said

After the film Tinker, Tailor (my title) was finished, I implored Major Ewart to let me get into action so, rather unwillingly, he gazetted me CO No 5 Independent Troop, Maritime RA (we had been given promotion as a force) to set up a shore base on Juno, the British Sector of the Second Front invasion, arriving at dawn on D+2. Our job was to service the weapons and gun crews of merchant ships involved in Overlord (the codename for the invasion), since it was expected that the fury of Hitler's air force would descend on them as they lay discharging cargoes off the beach-head.

One or two V-1 buzz-bombs (or doodlebugs) arrived, but so good was the Allied deception plan that Hitler firmly believed the main attack would come over the Pas de Calais and that Normandy was diversionary. Consequently, Goering's air force was irremediably held in reserve and the expected attacks on shipping did not occur.

This, and the holding back of tanks in the initial stages, undoubtedly contributed to the Allied success, which might well have been on a knife-edge otherwise.

As a result, when Montgomery liberated the East flank of the Allied break-out, No 5 Independent Troop eventually found itself stationed in Antwerp. Here there was more to do and there were V-1s and V-2s aplenty. One of the worst duties was recording survivors' accounts in our 'Action Reports'. As much detail as possible was vital – not only to the families but to Naval Intelligence. One horrific loss prompted this from me:

28. ON THE SINKING OF A TROOPSHIP

O lovers weep lest Love should weep alone,
For Love hath lost a thousand lives today.
How can our tears, how can our deeds atone?
How can our words say all there is to say?

These men were minded with a common aim;
They sailed the seas to keep a solemn trust;
They sought not praise, they sought not after fame;
They followed freedom: now their bodies rust.

These men were soldiers, some by conscript rote,
And some had chosen while there yet was choice;
But one and all proclaimed their country's vote
And death by drowning cannot still their voice.

O lovers, honour those who silent sleep
All hallowed in the hollow of the deep.

1945
Antwerp

The buzz-bombs sharpened one's perceptions of life. Feelings were strung tight and distraction was at a premium – even some pretty girl (perhaps romanticised in uniform) glimpsed across a room:

29. I KNOW NOT YOUR NAME

I know not your name,
But it's all the same,
For I love your eyes,
They are wide and wise
And your mouth is made
To be unafraid
If a man may kiss,
Believing in bliss.

You've a certain air
Of not being there,
Which sets you above
A commonplace love.
It's not far to seek
In the curve of cheek
And nostril meek.

Oh, the sun may shine
And the moonbeams meet
At my lady's shrine,
And there kiss her feet;
But she mayn't be mine,
For it is not meet.

October 1944

But perhaps restraint was broken. Then the inevitable lover's hangover:

30. THERE IS NO MORE A MORROW

Man is oft unbridled beast,
Who harkens not the marriage feast,
But leans toward the wanton.
True love he surely heeds the least,
For true love's wedded by the priest,
And wears a look that's lenten.

But when man gets his wilful way,
He's not content to learn and pay
The price of scented licence.
He needs must bribe his bartered soul
By filling up the begging bowl
Yet never can buy sense.

Until he reach the cold of dawn
And find himself marooned, forlorn
Upon the strand of sorrow.
Then shall he know the scourge of scorn,
That though this be another morn,
There is no more a morrow.

24 January 1945
Antwerp

In this lyric that follows I'm expressing the sadness of soul-mates who know that their love cannot survive. It is a passion that is fated from the first:

31. DESTINY

The words and the music tumble forth
As the flying train tears through the north,
With wheels whirling fast and miles flicking by
To the song of the rails and the sound of a sigh,
We cling there together, alone you and I.

With hearts beating madly to the rhythm of the rails,
Like the surf and the surge and the wind in the sails,
Aye, this is the journey, a journey to death
(Ah for some courage to save honour's breath)
For here all ends meet, the sea and the sky,
Darkness and light and, alone – you and I –
Like the mingling of dawn, like the matching of eve,
Which reconcile fact with make-believe.

So the track runs on till the twin rails meet –
Life and death in a time complete.

1945

The Allies were twisting their strangle-knot on the retreating Germans but Christmas '44 brought dire danger when von Runstedt launched a fierce desperation attack through the Ardennes, supported by many parachuted infiltrators in civilian garb or Allied uniform, that very nearly succeeded in piercing Montgomery's coastal flank. These parachutists almost caused my arrest. I was on my way back to Antwerp from a visit to Belgian friends, with whom I had been billeted in Alost whilst Montgomery's advance was temporarily stalled, when my Seep (amphibious jeep) was stopped at a checkpoint and my papers scrutinised. I was questioned fairly severely before being allowed to proceed. I think it was the Seep – and perhaps my unusual shoulder-flash, MRA around the shaft of a fouled anchor – that roused their suspicions.

This foray was supported by a New Year's Day lightning air strike on the port of Antwerp that really achieved very little.

Apart from this our days and nights were punctuated by the eerie 'drone- drone' of the buzz-bombs. Everybody listened acutely to the buzz-bombs. Once the noise cut out, you knew they were diving earthward to explode in about 15-20 seconds. If you heard the V-2s, you knew you had survived the explosion since their rate of fall was faster than the speed of sound.

The following impressions came to me in Antwerp:

32. SIDELIGHTS (GLIMPSED IN ANTWERP)

I THE DEVIL'S DUE!

When Adam milked the moon
And Eve enchanted earth
The Serpent sidled soon
And bought Behemoth's birth.

October 1944

" COR! "

II GRIEF ENCOUNTER

A woman at her window stood,
Weeping for her widowhood;
When as she watched a knight rode by,
Who waved at her. She wondered why
And, wondering, she dried her eye.

October 1944

III DEAD END

When youth is growing old
And fires are burning low;
When blood is running cold
And eye and limb are slow;
Then, take the knife and cut the life,
Yea Lord, let it be so.

13 March 1945

Not sure that in my 85th year I'd be wanting to say that:

IV NO? SERIOUSLY!

Heavy is the heart that sighs
And sees no solace,
But watches with unknowing eyes
The frolics and follies
Of all the facile folk who know not what hell is.

13 March 1945

In those youthful days soul-searching was almost a pastime, as witness this:

33. I'VE LOST MY YOUTH

I've lost my youth, the youth of former times;
My life is spent in making senseless rhymes,
Rhymes of this and that to divers names,
Names of the various loves whose listless claims
To my devotion weirdly wax or wane
Like dripping light reflected in a pane.

My youth was spent in striving for the stars
(The youth I had between the two great wars),
The stars that beckoned with beguiling eyes,
Whose looks belied their own indecent lies;
And many a star I found beyond my reach,
And many a toss and twist it took to teach
The rudiments of life, of thought and speech.

Still eager for the stars, I learned to doubt,
To think on this and reason that faith out,
To cast a stone at many an inbred creed;
Till, faced with fierce nostalgia's frantic need,
I sought to heal my heart in concrete clinic
And save my soul by crying, 'I'm a cynic!'

With the war in Europe over, Ewart posted me to Shoeburyness as adjutant to the 5th Maritime Regt RA, whose Colonel was Charles Lyttelton, the Worcestershire county cricket captain.

I enjoyed the cricket I was thrust into (one certainly didn't get weekend leave!), not having played since leaving school 11 years before. In the last game of the season – a blood match against Larkhill Gunnery School, an excellent side – as wicket-keeper I stood up to Lyttelton's county medium bowling. I had two catches and two stumpings, one off a yorker on the leg side, with which he was overjoyed. It was my dies mirabilis in a manner reminiscent of that gut-twisting verse from Newbolt's famous poem:

> There's a breathless hush in the Close tonight –
> Ten to make and the match to win –
> A bumping pitch and a blinding light,
> An hour to play and the last man in.

I was faced with the same situation but only one over to go before 'stumps'. Our ninth wicket fell to a catch at long leg off the last ball of the penultimate over. I'd crossed with the batsman before the catch was made, hoping that it would be dropped.

So, I faced the last over, with us still needing 10 and little comfort in having as partner Sgt Judd, who was excellent in Admin but not renowned as a No 11 batsman.

The first ball from their fast bowler, brought on to finish us off, provided an easy two into the covers. The second was similar. I could have taken three but the thought of my partner dissuaded me. The third was a beauty and I could do no more than play it respectfully. The fourth gave me only the chance of one but I knew I had to take it. So Sgt Judd faced the fifth. I summoned him to the middle and hissed, 'Sergeant, whatever happens to this ball, you run.' Looking scared, he nodded. As the bowler swung his arm, I was out of his crease and sprinting. The ball missed the stumps. The keeper, standing back, threw under-arm at the wicket. He missed but I was safely home anyway.

Last ball and four needed. It was fast, short of half-volley length. I swung my bat, hit it on the rise over the bowler's head for four runs! Drinks were on me in the Mess that night!

Lyttelton did me the honour of asking whether I'd be interested in playing for Worcestershire. I think he was serious, but now aged 30 and with a BBC career to resume, I sadly had to decline.

All this is by the way, as were these 'Fragments' that came to me that summer at Shoeburyness:

34. FRAGMENTS

I RATIONALE

The stringent sackcloth of our age,
The hairshirt of austerity.

II HOPE

A wild primrose with its promise of peace
And a permanent way of the heart.

III WINDSTREAMERS

The leaves of the trees
Are swimming in the breeze,
As if in swirling seas.
The swallow swift swings
In fitful flirting flings,
Flitting on flaunting wings.

IV   CAUSE AND EFFECT

Truth will out when love is dying,
And ruth is left in sorrow sighing.

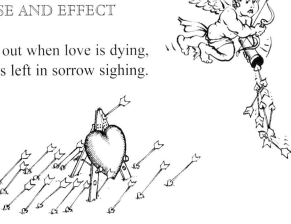

V   HANGOVER

But after night
There comes the dawn
And after dawn, the morrow ...
Then woeful wight,
Marooned forlorn
Upon the rock of sorrow

1945-6
Shoeburyness

My next was inspired by The Times *Competition No 843. The exact rules I don't remember and, of course, I didn't win: 'Mr S. apologises to those friends he was prevented from saying goodbye to on Saturday.' (Entry in* The Times *personal column, c 1946):*

35. FAITHFUL MR SOLE

Old Sole he was a careful man,
A traveller beside,
But he fell out with Reaper Time,
Untimely reaped he died.

For he'd arranged to meet some friends,
'Ere sailing to Cathay,
But on his way to fête his mates,
Fate mated him this way.

Dear Sole, who always crossed his cheques,
Was checked at Charing Cross;
On Jehu Jones, a taxi-man,
The jury laid his loss.

Before Sole died, lest friends should carp,
He left this last adieu;
Then hastened heavenward with harp
To play a scale or two.

1946

I had now separated from Nancy and was burying myself in work, as a producer and commentator in the European Service. I was also writing quite a lot of verse. The next three show the way my feelings were conjuring:

36. A GLEAM OF GOLD

My troubled thoughts are quietened now
And stilled by whispering fire;
The quietude of evening's brow,
Serene without desire.

For all the day life's turgid stream
Has slurred along its course;
And how much happier is my dream
When forged with firelight's force.

I dream a dream of lover's bliss
And thought of poet's mould,
And as I ponder this and this
I glimpse a gleam of gold.

1946

37. EVENTIDE

I sit alone as evening falls,
Forgotten are the weary walls
Of blank civilisation.
I only hear the drowsy calls
Of birds a-bedding
And watch twilight spreading
Over all. Each at his station
Enjoys relief from drums of day
And servitude to pending tray,
Release and peace.

1946

38. EVENING PRAYER

The evening wind bestirs the grass
That softly parts to let me pass.
The silver clouds mount in the west,
The robin settles to its nest.
The restless sea creeps o'er the sand ...
Oh that my love were by my hand.

The end of the war saw civilisation's saviour, Winston Churchill, and the Tories ousted by a new electorate that found its voice in the aftermath. It was as great a triumph for Labour as the 1997 election – some 50 years on.

However, it was not easy for the new government who faced the sacrifices made for victory: a huge debt, the trade balance with the USA heavily in America's favour and no rich pickings to make a war-worn public happier. Shortages and austerity were the order of the day. Britain was sliding down a greasy pole with the flames seemingly overwhelming.

Yet, in a positive frame of mind I was more optimistic:

39. DECLINE?

They say that Britain's lost her pride of place
And bows to newer nations' will to war;
The thin red line has been stretched out too far,
Her hand no longer holds the mighty mace
Of world dominion; run for her the race:
Or so they say, who claim to know the law,
Which loves to lavish those who have with more
And 'gainst the weaker brethren turns its face.

But I believe her glories are not gone,
That she has yet a greater goal to gain,
A loftier leadership for her attain.
When peace is woven, thornéd crown is won,
Then from the loins of war shall seed a son
Begat of Tory grief and Labour pain.

1946

I often went home to the apple farm at Great Totham and would sometimes go walking by myself, trying to work out the whys and wherefores of life. One day I came across a donkey:

40. DONKEY SERENADE

Alone I sat, alone I sat
And gazed at a donkey nigh
A wise old moke, I thought, and fat,
And comfort in his eye.

'Old ass,' I said, 'Old ass,' I said,
'You've seen the seasons fly;
You've bored yourself on many a bed;
Dost know the where and why?'

'Don't say me nay, don't say me nay,'
And I heaved a heavy sigh.
But mute he stood as if to pray
And would not meet my eye.

I sat alone, I sat alone.
A vacant ass stood by:
But nature deftly did atone
With sight of sea and sky.

August 1946

It was a similar sort of experience that inspired:

41. SNAIL TRAIL

As we watch the sluggish snail
Slowly slime its shiny trail
There's only one thing we bewail –
That it cannot wag its tail.

Some men seek the Holy Grail;
Others vie for beauty's veil;
Some prefer a pint of ale:
But we are pleased to watch the snail.

The snail, the snail, the soothing snail!
In ecstasies that never stale
We watch on down, we watch in dale
The squirmings of the squamous snail.

17 September 1946

By now Nancy and I were divorced and I was doing what at 22 I had missed by marrying as an inexperienced innocent. As a reasonable looker and working for radio and television, it was not difficult to have friends amongst attractive girls but, for the present, it went no further than that.

One of our post-war tribulations was to suffer many power cuts. The following facetious Valentine was somehow contrived:

42. VALENTINE 1947

My beauteous Felicity
I strive with every art
By intermittent electricity
To translate my missing heart.

The light of love is strong despite ...
Why, that's peculiar!
The evanescent image mirrored bright
Is pretty Julia ...

Now glides Belinda's lissom form,
Endowed by candlelight,
An incandescent souvenir of norm
And love at any sight ...

But who? Oh yes, Felicity,
Forgive this song in part,
Reverberating eccentricity
Of light and hollow heart.

(I never had a girl friend with any of those names.)

13 February 1947

Alas, bureaucracy, so prevalent today, began then to make its weight felt even more than during wartime rationing, as particularly portrayed in that brilliant backs-to-the-wall TV series, Dad's Army. I was moved to indict it – bureaucracy that is:

43. THE BUREAUCRAT

I am one of those gentlemen,
Complacent and stout,
One of those with a governing nose,
Who says, 'Go without.'

Pleased and patently pleasing,
Improvident, blind.
This is the day, hip, hip, hooray!
Of me and my kind.

Ours is the slave-grave new world,
Grey and forbidding.
Social advance, success without chance,
Enterprise ridding!

All kinds of form our métier –
We never get stuck.
Ours to conflict, ours to restrict –
And pass on the buck.

I am one of those gentlemen
Whom morons cherish.
Long live the fool to put up with my rule!
May neither perish.

April 1947

The European Service gave me an invaluable experience of commentating and interviewing on any subject in the news. Being staff and therefore free of fee, I was also being used more and more by the newly burgeoning TV Outside Broadcasts and I was getting the odd freelance job. For one of these I was put up with local BBC contacts. They were a most delightful family whose surname, alas, I cannot now remember:

44. THE LODGE, LANCHESTER

Harold's mark at golf is par
And he's wizard with a car;
Alice drives a steady course,
But much prefers to ride a horse;
Mother keeps the garden trim,
Indulging thus her 'crazy' whim;
George delights in gnawing bones
And litt'ring rooms with errant stones;
A nicer household hard to find,
Where each may do and speak his mind.

May 1947

In retrospect it is easy to be cynical and come up with cryptic titles. At the time of writing, sincerity is all:

45. ILLUSION

The train is bearing me toward my Love
And fast doth beat my heart,
If wheels could only faster move
And play their part.

My Love will greet me in the starry light
And I shall feel her form,
Her loveliness half hid by night,
Her kisses warm.

Each day shall find us further steeped in love,
And blest shall we be both,
Renewing with the power above
Our true love troth.

Oh, we shall know the beauty and the peace
The single-hearted find,
A gentle loving without cease,
A certain mind.

September 1947

A pair of sweet girls became friends of mine. Neither did I pursue seriously. Rosemary was doing a shorthand course and was nervous of the Principal:

46. SHORTHAND SONG

Sweet Rosemary, so lovely, kind
So courteous and brave;
A shorthand crotchet? Never mind,
Take minim and/or stave.

Endowed with virtue's shining gift,
Fear not the tyrant's ire,
For dragons fume with fretful shrift,
But frizzle under fire.

For here's one true puts trust in you
And knows you labour long,
So have at her whate'er you do
And tilt a sally song.

And if the thought should cross your mind
'Has he his tongue in cheek?'
Cast out such sentiment unkind,
My eye is mild and meek.

23 January 1948

Most women are far better letter-writers than men. I have early memories of my mother always with a pad on her knee, even when rollicking along in a turbulent train. I soon became aware that women loved the exclamation mark as a friend in expressive need:

"ow!"

47. !!!

Sometimes the surge of inward strife
Demands an outlet; feelings rife
That man would turn to instant 'damn!'
A woman must contain like lamb
Or lose her name for ladyhood
(And that I'm sure she never could).
Then, better still than bite or bark
The simple exclamation mark.

The mark, the mark, the vicious mark,
The merely meretricious mark,
The sneery-beery snigger mark,
The finger-on-the-trigger mark,
The brighter and the bigger mark –
All these and divers other stark
Downstrokes and blobs denote the mark.

Some sages like to emphasise
Their triter truths – and oft their lies –
With underlines in slashes bold
(To warm the words that sound too cold).
Italics too or thicker type
Lend stuffing to enrich their tripe.

But if you really must impress
And give your sentiments due stress
Then use the exclamation mark,
The sheer exasperation mark –
You'll make your meaning plain, I guess!

9 March 1948

Lawn tennis had already become a regular factor in my life. In those early post-war days, the Bournemouth Hard Court Championships were regarded as the unofficial national title – and we had some good players! One Sunday, after covering the finals, I was returning to London to play for the BBC cricket team at Motspur Park. Here I describe scenes glimpsed en passant through the carriage window:

48. OUTWARD GLIMPSE

I woke to the sound of the restless sea
And footsteps faltering by,
I lay and listened awhile to the dree
Of the gulls' unearthly cry.

I broke my fast in the rollicking train
And heeded the countryside.
A gang of children used the mane
Of a hayrick as a slide.

A cricket field lay green in the sun,
Whose rays in the dew still played.
The groundsman gazed at work well done
And a careful wicket laid.

Then came a church's lance-head spire,
Aglint for a new crusade;
Then the wharves and quays and a port's full choir
Of cranes with uplift aid.

The relentless wheels went whirling on
And landscape shifting by ...
The country soon gave way to town
And pressing purpose nigh.

2 May 1948
Bournemouth to London

1948. The cricket season had just started with the touring side's opening match against Lancashire. Don Bradman was captaining the Aussies in his last Test Series. Lancashire had beaten them on a 'sticky':

49. TESTY WICKET

When Bad Man
Bradman
Attacked the men of Lancs,
They built on
M Hilton
Who earned his county's thanks.

And Red Rose
Sped close
To equalling White's deed;
A bright note,
The right note
In the hour of England's need.

So here's to Smailes and Hilton
Who've proved that idols may,
When caught on sticky wickets,
Develop feet of clay.

May Bradman and Hasset,
May Miller and McCool,
Be humbled in their heyday
And learn the ancient rule
That, come a common enemy,
The men of York and Lancs
Forget their champion quarrel
And conspire to close their ranks.

So Bad Man
Bradman,
'Ware the opening day!
Sticky wicket,
Why, that's cricket!
That's the way we like to play.

1948

Two interesting girls (one a BBC producer) I knew at this time are pictured in my next two verses:

50. D I

D stands for Doyle – Suzanne of that ilk,
As pretty as pearls, as sleek as is silk.
For her thesis she reads in the British Museum
With marked Disziplin and great ENTHUSEUM.
Cooking and housework she won't do for toffee,
But she packs a strong punch and boy she makes coffee!
This Lorelei shines aloft on her perch,
But alas she is lost above clouds of research.

31 October 1948

51. D II

D stands for Doncaster – Caryl by name,
Who thinks that her Reason will open Sesame;
But how to pronounce it she hasn't a notion
Till instinct contrives to give vein to emotion.
Then, you'll agree, she needs no instruction
In making the best, the art of production.
Yes, I give her full marks for her light-fingered cooking,
But I bet she throws plates when there's nobody looking!

31 October 1948

It was in 1948 that I met Liza. I was once again gauleiter of a European gaggle of reporters from the various language services sent to cover the Conservative Party Conference at the Brighton Dome. Having done my piece for the English Service, I (being no dancer) was hanging about the fringe of a cocktail-dansant organised for the Press. Before I knew what was happening I found myself whisked onto the dance floor by a very attractive girl – Liza. She was working for Central Office and her boss had said to her, 'Do something about that misery from the BBC.' Within a few months we were married.

I was now virtually into my 'Blank Age' as far as writing verse was concerned. As for work, I was never out of it, being constantly in demand with the BBC's post-war expansion of TV and also Radio programmes.

I was chairman of the original Panorama; hosted quiz shows and children's programmes; made two series of travel programmes with Liza in Australia and the West Indies; was constantly used as a reporter/interviewer on sporting programmes; and became the first Winter Sports commentator. I also covered 11 Winter and Summer Olympics; and Wimbledon every year.

I was too busy and fulfilled to pursue versifying, though the next poem, which was published in Ariel, the BBC house magazine, was written a year or so after I had left the European Service to join the Outside Broadcasts Department, headed by the formidable mind and 6ft 7in figure of Seymour de Lotbinière, known to all as Lobby.

Lobby dissected our programmes – especially our commentaries – with a fine mental scalpel; and you knew you'd get away with nothing. However approving he might appear to be to start with, you waited for the dreaded, 'But I didn't quite understand ... ' followed by a series of valid points. That was maddening, just the sheer inevitability. If you were honest with yourself, you knew he was right. But you always wanted desperately to do your best for him.

I was on the establishment as a producer/commentator so that one was constantly concerned with the fore and aft of an Outside Broadcast. This time I was the producer and No 2 to Wynford Vaughan

Thomas, whose Welsh gift for gusto and imagery never failed to bring a commentary alive. On this occasion he did more than that.

Rising to a climax, Wynford said, 'And now the trumpets shrill ... The doors are flung wide ... and there enters that most loved, that most gracious figure, His Majesty ... Queen Mary!'

I never mentioned it, nor did he. I suspect that mentally he'd been expecting to see the King and Queen, forgetting that Queen Mary, the Queen Mother, would come first.

This was probably the last great state occasion that could not be covered by the fledgling Television Service, which only just got the necessary complement of OB cameras and production equipment in time for the Queen's Coronation in 1953. What we were now witnessing was a joint celebration of the 900th anniversary of the building of Westminster Hall and the refurbishment of the Chamber of the House of Commons, which had been hit by a bomb during the war.

It was a great patriotic event, which had one unexpected light side at the very beginning:

52. STATE OCCASION

Not a pin was heard
And nobody stirred,
But all sat primly in great Expectation.
For from far and wide
And on every side
Were gathered the Great of this great little nation.

Were gathered the Great
In pomp and in state
To solemnly sit and patiently wait.

Of a sudden a stir
And a whispered spur –
Then thrill of trumpet proclaiming procession.
First came the Mace
With due pride of place
And the Chancellor followed in simple progression.

Through the ranks of the Great
On carpet of state
He measuredly marched with dignified gait.

Then plain to the view
Were the marks of his shoe
As he proudly paced in slow graduation,
A slur on the hue
Of that surroyal blue
Far worse than any rude expectoration.

'Tween the ranks of the Great
That slow measured gait
Left dusty imprints on the carpet of state.

But no sooner seen
Than rushed ladies in green,
Determined that nothing should mar such occasion:
A task force to clean
They swept through the scene,
A startling and swift Amazonian invasion.

Midst the smiles of the Great,
In the nick of 'too late',
They furiously swept the carpet of state ...

Then, unsullied and clean,
That carpet serene
Was fit once more for the foot of a queen.

And while Majesty moved in panoply proud
Through the ranks of the Great whose heads humbly bowed,
While loyal addresses were read out aloud
And ancient fealty was once more avowed ...

Blushing unseen,
With pride and with preen,
Watched those heavenly bodies, the ladies in green.

Westminster Hall
October 1950

And that was almost the last poem, of which I have any record, that I wrote in what I suppose might be loosely termed my 'Lyric Period'. Then, for 40 years I wrote nothing, largely because I was fulfilled with BBC work for TV and Radio, especially my annual jamboree at Wimbledon. Latterly, when work was sliding away, and I was in living in Alderney, I was for some time extremely unhappy – not a frame of mind conducive to writing. For me it was my 'Stoic' or 'Blank Age'.

There are two exceptions. When the following was written in 1973, I was a Lord's Taverner and contributed this to a Presentation Book being given to Dorothy Carline. She had introduced me to contact lenses which I tried for a time:

53. DOROTHY CARLINE

Dear darling Dorothy (Carline)
No empathy nor skill of mine
Could wholly glean or yet divine
The sovereign goodness that we know,
Which gathered gifts from high and low,
Sing Taverner and tombelow.

Our love and thanks are ever thine
But I who see with new found eyen
Of contact known through your design
Will sing the praises to and fro
Of Dorothy to whom I owe
Lens sana in oculo sano.

Apart from Wimbledon, my favourite job for many years was being presenter, or Chairman as the job was then called, of Going for a Song, the first TV programme devoted to antiques. It ran from 1964 to '77 (and has now been revived on daytime TV with a different format) with a break of three years two-thirds of the way through.

The panjandrum of the programme, Arthur Negus, had a tremendous TV following. Viewers loved to see him caressing furniture, his favourite subject, though as cataloguer for a well-known county auctioneers he had a wide expertise and sure eye. Fortunately, he knew nothing about Oriental Art, so my slight knowledge gained his respect. This was useful, for Arthur could be 'arkard' if you got up against him.

As it was, we became friends and I edited his book, Going For A Song – English Furniture, Arthur Negus Talks to Max Robertson.

And now for my second exception to my 'Blank Age'. The assistant editor of Going for a Song was Paul Smith, who was good at writing song music. We combined our efforts in 'The Love Match' which, alas, did not find a publisher. Here now are the words I wrote:

54. THE LOVE MATCH

" **LOVE ALL !** "

We met in a love match
By luck of the draw;
You made me unsteady
Before I could score.

Cupid: Are you ready?

Our match was uneven
From the love-all start;
With Cupid as umpire
I soon lost all heart.

Cupid: Play!

You won every rally,
You won every game;
Set, and five love
Soon stood to your name.

Cupid: Love thirty!

I served to recover,
You sensed I was done;
Strive as I might
I knew you had won.

Cupid: Love forty!

With match-point against me,
I'd left it too late;
And you were the winner,
I found with my Fate.

Cupid: Game, Set and Match!

We met in a love match
– My luck in the draw –
And now I'm quite ready
To settle the score.

" YOU WIN ! "

Liza and I had separated when I left Alderney in '84 to live for a while in Guernsey and we were divorced a year or two later. It was in Guernsey that I met Pat Savill in 1986, just before my last Wimbledon fortnight as a BBC commentator. We got on well most of the time, punctuated by furious clashes of our artistic temperaments. Having sold our houses at about the same time in 1989, we decided to travel together.

On our way down to Cap Ferrat on the Côte d'Azur, we had paused for a day or two in Normandy. There we met Françoise, a skilled restorer of old pictures, and of course her techniques were fascinating to Pat who had studied art for six years:

55. FRANÇOISE, RESTAURATRICE NONPAREILLE

Sweet cleanser of the art and soul of man,
Who maketh whole the canvas of his life,
Teasing the fretted strands befrayed by strife
To patterned scheme that once again doth scan.

Next comes the arcane work of paint repair,
Applying hue on hue of secret dyes,
Each deftly mixed and laid in olden wise
Completely to confound the connoiss-air.

And now her skill doth flow with brilliant scope
To bright the pallid pigments wan through time
And recreate their former 'gloire' sublime,
Reviving pride that blazons forth new hope.

The rebirth done, remains but one more part,
The final vernissage to heighten art.

December 1991
Normandy

I had also been very moved by the death of an old friend, Cuthbert Bell, a largely self-taught – perhaps slightly dilettante – artist, who late in life was developing well and beginning to have some success. He lived in Suffolk and loved the East Anglian landscapes, especially the coastal fringes. His favourite subject was a beach with the sea beyond and an impressive sunset or sunrise as background.

We made friends and I became a patron, buying far too many of his pictures, for which there was never enough room later in my Wimbledon flat. I had often been supported by Christine on the air and was grateful when she and Gerry Janes came to my rescue, buying the largest and best pair. I'm so glad that they've gone where they are really appreciated – to their appropriate home on the East Coast.

I knew Cuthbert was dying of cancer when I opened his last exhibition. On news of his death, I was in Cap Ferrat. This was the first poem I wrote there:

56. IN MEMORIAM CUTHBERT BELL

Tonight I saw a sky of vivid hue,
Suffused with shades of pink and green and blue,
So delicate in opalescent glow,
I knew the sight most rending I had seen,
Just as your evening sketches used to show –
The blending colours held in fading sheen.

You loved the loneliness of sky beset
With evanescent lights of life's sun set.
You dreamt the ever-stretching shadowed dream
That carried soul away from scarring strife
Toward the brightly beckoning wayward gleam
That was the constant beacon of your life.

Now that your sky has set, Divinity
Shall lead you forth toward infinity.

It wasn't long before I heard that John Arlott had died. We were still in Cap Ferrat when news of his death broke. He had moved to Alderney when I was living there. I had seen very little of him during our working careers, for we covered different sports. In Alderney I got to know him much better and enjoyed drinking wine with him. I wanted to give him an epitaph:

57. FOR JOHN

Consider all the names that spring to mind
When cricket is the subject of mankind.
There's Grace, of course, et sequitur there's Hobbs
Bradman, Botham, Lindwall, Miller – Larwood
And all the rest of cricket pageant's nobs,
Whose skill was legend with the ball or wood.

But solely quintessential to the game
That loved, revered and illustrious name:

ARLOTT.

" ... AND HE'S COMING IN TO BOWL ...! "

It was in Cap Ferrat at a private zoo that Pat and I witnessed an enthralling and terrifying sight:

58. TIGER, TIGER, SLEEPING TIGHT?

Two tigers lay gaoled, surrendered to rue,
Bengal's striped nabobs barred in a zoo;
Magnificent beasts with nothing to do
Save acquiesce with inquisitive view,
Glazing their eyes with supine indolence,
Scornful display of royal indifference.

Five pigeons alighted, curtsied and cooed,
Pertly subscribing a shifting of mood ...
Of a sudden one tiger reared and struck
Its reach overwhelming, its paws amok
As they slashed at the frantic fluttering brood ...
And a carpet of feathers soon lay strewed.

The squall of violence and fear having died,
The tiger went back to its sleep belied.

12 January 1992
Cap Ferrat

Pat Savill is by birth and skill an artist. Born and brought up in Staffordshire, she was first a teacher of art before going for three years to the Ruskin at Oxford. She and her fellows were the guinea-pigs who enabled the Ruskin to make the following year a degree course.

The garden of the cottage we had in Cap Ferrat was an ideal spot for her to get down to painting. I dug my trench in the dining room. If she came though to the kitchen, asking 'Like a cup of coffee?' or 'Shall we go for a walk?' I was always busy scribbling, so inevitably I produced some verse. The tribute to John Arlott and 'Tiger, Tiger' were the first two in what I think of as my 'Ironic Age'.

As I said, they could be tempestuous times:

59. THE ARTIST FRAMED

She had painted fast with controlled passion
A still life of apples, vase and flowers,
Vibrant with colour and well balanced powers,
Exciting to glimpse her quick skill to fashion.

Suddenly certainty dissolved in doubt.
'Oh, it's a mess! I'm not a real artist!'
'You are, you know; it's where your true heart is.'
'Don't be stupid! You know nothing!' (a shout).

'May as well see what it's like in a frame.'
Much discussion flows on colour and mount.
The framer's experience provides the fount
And brings into focus the artist's aim.

The final result is certainly good.
'I *am* an artist!' in exultant mood.

17 January 1992
Cap Ferrat

60. WHEN LOVE DIED

When love died
I sighed
And cried.
When respect bowed
I vowed
Never
Ever
Again –
Too much pain …
But I lied.

19 January 1992
Cap Ferrat

It was in February, whilst we were at the cottage, that Her Majesty the Queen announced that she would never abdicate and a week later Dan Maskell let it be known that he was retiring. This prompted the following:

61. DECISION DAYS

When the Queen of the realm decides to stay,
But the King of tennis calls it a day,
'Oh, I say! Oh, I say!'

Now Maskell has quit the commentary box
The rest will have to pull up their socks,
Or take a few knocks – quite a few knocks.

How to compete with a living legend?
There's only one way. You take the pledge and ...
Now where do you stand? Where do you stand?

Well, you do your homework – six hours a day,
And then you go out and describe the play.
'Oh, I say! Oh, I say!'

Cap Ferrat
7 February 1992

Worried that Dan and his followers might think that this trivialised him and his work, I followed up more seriously:

62. TO DAN

It takes a brave and sage man to retire,
The going still so good, the world your crown;
When, spite the traps and trappings of renown
With all their glitter, you still have your fire.

But, Dan, you are that 'rara avis' man,
Single of purpose and upright of mind,
Knowledgeable, so courteous, always kind,
Working at life while measuring the span.

Your famous dictum will be sorely missed,
Your fans will often find their screens go blank,
As in mind's eye each plays his mem'ry bank,
Hearing your voice unerring in the gist.

Whatever target you shall now essay,
Their response will always be 'Oh, I say!'

7 February 1992
Cap Ferrat

A day or two later I wrote the following sonnet for the Queen, whose sense of service to her subjects shines out as a beacon of nationhood:

63. REGINA CUM LAUDE

For forty years since first acknowledged Queen,
Public exemplar at each crisis hour
Of history, not strife nor ebbing pow'r
Has seen her falter from her way serene.

Above yet cognisant of cross debate,
She's ever guardian of the nation's conscience,
The nucleus that generates and hence
Spurs any laggard leaders of the state.

Her sense of service is the bright lodestar
By which she metes both commoners and kings.
To all the pomp and circumstance she brings
A dignity that malice cannot mar.

Her paradigm, a beacon, shines transcendent,
Majesty untarnished and resplendent.

February 1992
Cap Ferrat

A year later found us installed in a lovely Queen Anne house Pat had bought at Aldbourne, a village half way between Swindon and Hungerford. I was determined to keep on writing verse but found my mind in something of a vacuum – with this result:

64. CLEAN SHEET

With mind and memory wiped clean,
What's left of life should seem serene
But Future wings to steal the scene.
The brain at once begins to thunder
Gem-precious plans for pirates' plunder
And evil men to rend asunder.

The spring of thought anew to flow
From sun-parched source of up-and-go
Dribbles along ... but ... oh... so ... slow!
Desperate need of word elation
And joyous height of jubilation
Seeks remedy from inspiration.

Elusive muse so false to find
That leaves my nucleus entwined,
So fickle to my pleading mind:
My soul sighs deep for sorrow's unction
But thou hast not the least compunction.
If only one small cell would function!

One tiny gleam to light the way
With all my heart for it I pray –
Just something sensible to say:
But fate is stern: 'You may well whistle
Or sing a song aping the missel,
Yet each will gain but just dismissal.'

October 1993
Aldbourne

At least I drew some inspiration from an attractive Christmas card we were sent:

65. MAL DE MERMAID

The mermaid sat and scanned the sea
From rocky shelf of promont'ry,
'Where is my Love, oh, where is he?
This year, next year, when shall it be?
Dear Neptune, bring Merman to me.'

December 1993
Aldbourne

It was while at Aldbourne that a partial collapse led to a searching examination and I was fortunate to be referred to the famous Oxford heart hospital, the Radcliffe. I'd had a pacemaker fitted some years before while in Guernsey but it was now found that I needed a double bypass and a new aortic valve. I shall always be grateful to the American pig that provided this aortic valve and so far it has performed faultlessly. Dr Oliver Ormerod, in medical charge of the Heart Department, told me at my annual inspection last year that normally with his stethoscope he knew at once the difference between a pig's and a human aortic valve but that with mine he couldn't tell. I'm not certain what this says about me but I find it very reassuring.

The nurses in the cardiac ward were superb:

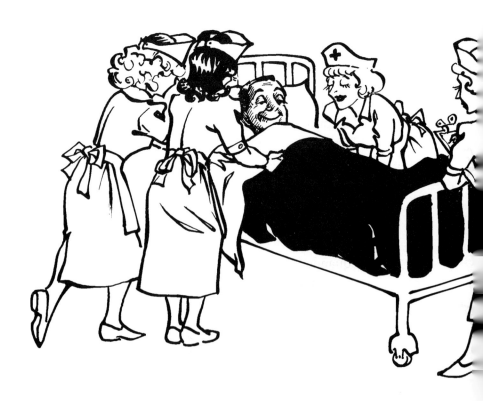

66. TO 5 D – CARDIAC WARD

Angels minist'ring our plight,
Soothers in the dread of night,
Each more lovely than the last
(Sighing regret for what is past),
It's no surprise we fall in love,
With visions largessed from above.

The day is set for surgeon's knife,
Will it be death or yet more life?
The solace shown e'en greater now
That hand is nailed unto the plough.

The deed is done, the furrows stitched,
The heed still sweet but subtly switched:
The purpose now to make and mend,
To give the patient will to fend
Himself against misfortune's tide,
To earn respect and take back pride.

Till finally angelic care
Just simply is no longer there –
Squandered instead on upstarts new.
High time indeed to bid 'adieu'!

July-August 1994
Aldbourne

Whilst at Aldbourne, I paid more than one visit to old friends, Peter and Fay Cairns, who live at Berkswell, near Coventry. Peter and I had first met when we often worked together in the early days of postwar television. He was with the BBC in Birmingham and it wasn't long before I was invited to his home and met Fay:

67. PETER AND FAY CAIRNS

They must have been the fairest bairns,
Dear Peter and his Fay – the Cairns:
He steady Virgo resolute,
She, Leo lass who gives no hoot
But hurtles through in brilliant style,
Leaving a wake of winning smile.
A truly harnessed team these two,
Top names in any 'Friends Who's Who'.

2 September 1994
Aldbourne

Another old friend and working colleague over many Wimbledon years was Christine Truman, whose husband, Jerry Janes, had also been at Haileybury. Christine, as in her play, was thoughtful, decisive and not backward in expressing her viewpoint. We were often teamed together and enjoyed our verbal sparring on the air, as apparently listeners did. This is a polish-up of what I wrote in 1986 – my last Wimbledon for the BBC.

Christine was with me at the time – in the box – but we were not on the air:

68. CHRISTINE TRUMAN JANES

Oh, Christine dear where have you been –
In thought and word not on the scene?
We hear your deep and heartstrung sighs
And know you notice Bobo's thighs.
What splendid glistening limbs they are,
Like tree trunks hinting at his power!
What marvellous poise and grand design
Apparent in his kindling mien!
And when those thund'rous serves destroy
The best of men, we see your joy
And sense your pulse-rate rise within
Your glorious form, oh dear Christine.

4 September 1994
Aldbourne

Of course, 'Bobo' was Slobodan Zivojinovic. The original of this was written, I think, during my last BBC Wimbledon in 1986. It is in my 1986 Wimbledon Memorabilia file, together with a verse that Chris wrote of me.

The name of Fred Perry is the brightest beacon in the annals of British tennis at New Wimbledon. As a glorious past champion and superb reader of tactics, he was a long-time colleague in the commentary box.

Fred was a natural rebel. Son of a Labour MP, he brushed aside the stiff-lipped opposition of those who thought him a 'bounder'. He was a 'bounder' by snob standards of the day. He wanted to win; he hated to lose and certainly practised a highly developed gamesmanship. How unsporting can you be?

But aren't we all bounders in one way or another – especially now when selfishness is the order of the day? In Fred's case the word 'bounder' brings to my mind his leap of the net to shake the hand and further overwhelm the spirit of his victim.

To me he was a loyal friend who interrupted his schedule on a busy world tour to attend the farewell dinner BBC Outside Broadcasts gave me in 1986.

Fred, already a junior champion at table tennis (world champion at 19) first became aware of lawn tennis aged 14, when he and his father were on holiday at Eastbourne. Hearing interesting sounds behind the granite walls of Devonshire Park, Fred had to look. It was a glimpse of fate:

69. TO FRED PERRY (1909-1995)

You heard the siren call of ball on string,
So dared to scale the wall of Devon Park;
You stared as white-clad figures made their mark
And knew your heart was lost and soul would sing.

You leapt the barricades of barren 'form'
And strode the tennis courts in conqu'ring mode.
For you the goal was set and straight the road,
The rule to fight with gut and not conform.

Your chafing spirit seized its proud reward
As overlord supreme, acknowledged Champion,
Receiving pulsing plaudits from the Pantheon,
Thrice-running victor on All England sward.

You stand there rightful guardian of the shrine:
May patriotic fame be ever thine.

Aldbourne
2 February 1995

*That I wrote in Aldbourne the day Fred died in Melbourne, as a result
of a typical Perry gesture. He slipped and fell over the edge of the bath
when getting ready for a dinner in honour of Ken Rosewall during the
Australian Championships. He was in great pain with cracked ribs but
insisted on attending and only later was admitted to hospital where he
developed pneumonia.*

As I wrote, I knew he was dying.

Many of the subjects for my verses have sprung from items in The Daily Telegraph, *especially when eagerly and expensively perused overseas. A column I try not to miss is Donald Trelford's 'Talking Sport' on Tuesdays. On 1 December 1994, he discussed the evidence his readers had provided as to whether Sherlock Holmes's side-kick, Dr Watson, had played for Rosslyn Park or the Harlequins. I sent him the following, of which he only had space for the first verse only:*

70. ELEMENTARY, MY DEAR TRELFORD

Did Watson play for Rosslyn Park
Or bear the colours of Blackheath?
'Tis much the same as hunting snark –
An arcane problem for belief.

When genius strikes, the mind to bend,
All lesser folk shall stand in awe,
Just praying its bounty will descend
As marvel manna evermore.

So Watson, Holmes, Dodgson and Doyle
Will always be synonymous
With myth and mirth as fallow foil
To tedium's barren animus.

Aldbourne
1 December 1994

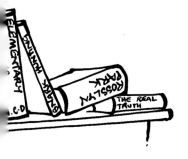

At the same time he quoted my tribute to Brian Johnston, whose death had saddened so many:

71. ENVOI TO BJ

Johners
Shone upon us...
Now he's goners.

An old friend – and a very good versifier – Buzzer Hadingham enjoyed his 80th birthday at this time. He'd had a very distinguished career as Chairman of Slazengers, Sparks and the All England Club. This was written in birthday acclaim:

72. REMEMBER, REMEMBER THE SIXTH OF DECEMBER

Dear Buzz, despite you've made sparks fly
And pulled the strings of many a racket,
You have my vote as the kinda guy,
For whom I'd always tick the placet.

Now you've attained a wiser state
And turn your thoughts to matters weighty,
I feel I may congratulate
A fellow fool who has made eighty.

But not enough to beat retreat
And stand in fighting rearguard action,
The wider aim, a finer feat,
To show life still has great attraction.

So here's to ninety – e'en a cent'ry!
We'll sing a song in celebration,
Until we reach the final sentry,
Who says, 'Pass friend – it's destination.'

Aldbourne
5 December 1995

137

Within a year of Fred Perry's death, the tennis world lost another familiar figure, Roy McKelvie, the Daily Mail's *correspondent, who latterly had been the doyen of the Wimbledon Press and liaison officer with the All England Club. We were both keen club cricketers as opening batsmen/wicket-keepers. Although a late post-war newcomer to the game, he'd also joined me as a partner in a minor rackets championship.*

This came naturally and I was able to read it at his funeral.

73. ROY

Named as a king, you were always the sort
To act with whole heart in your work or sport.
You lived your life through with gusto and guts:
In argument you could drive someone nuts.

At cricket too, you rejoiced as a stumper;
As partner in need you were never a dumper.
You fully believed that life should be fun –
The first to subscribe – why you were the one.

You always reviewed straight from the shoulder,
But would not allow malice to smoulder.
Where someone deserved it, you would give praise;
But, if ill-doers, you'd chastise their ways.

'Twas not your habit to please ev'ry one,
But all of us loved you, son of a gun.

5 January 1996
Aldbourne

My last piece of verse at Aldbourne was the cry of the damned. For some years I had been suffering with Trigeminal Neuralgia, an excruciating nerve pain in the face. I had reached the point when it was recurring too often. I was referred to a lady specialist, whose name was shortened by everyone to Dr Zak. She felt she was getting near the truth of this wicked torment. She referred me to her boss, Professor Paul Bradley who, by cutting a piece out of the nerve, was able to give me relief for 18 months. Then the nerve rejoined and the pain returned acutely.

Since then a neuro-surgeon, Peter Hamlyn, to whom Paul sent me, has electronically cauterised the nerve and brought blessed relief. But for how long? He can't say, though there's a good chance that it is for at least two years. Now – apart from my age – it's perhaps understandable why I'm in such a hurry to get this book finished and my reading recorded:

74. TRIGEMINAL NEURALGIA

Trigeminal or Triterminal –
For that's what it feels like
With its forked lightning strike
That drives me dumb with pain interminal.

We feel it here, we feel it there,
We feel it sometimes God knows where.
This devil's fork with lightning twist
Of paralysing force, its fist
So brutal as to cause me mix
My metaphors and oft-time fix
My being frozen in a pose
So rigid, like to bite my nose.

Pity Trigeminal Neuralgia,
That Pimpernel of Pain;
For Zak is on its track,
Determined to ease the strain.

Pimpernel pain, beware! Beware!
Prepare to cower in your lair,
Be it in lower or upper jaw –
Or more mysterious – far, far more –
Be it located in the brain,
The source of all this futile pain,
'Tis no matter, for Great Sleuth Zak
Is getting closer. She's on your track!

21 February 1996
Aldbourne

" GOTCHA! "

Pat and I found that life at 'The Big House' wasn't working. Neither of us – I especially – was the partying type and I was finding I couldn't really afford my half of the upkeep. So the house was sold and we went our ways, though continuing to see each other.

For 15 months I had a seventh-floor flat in one of the two big blocks overlooking Wimbledon. It was a fascinating time to have this privileged view, for the new No 1 Court was being built and I witnessed the whole process from the stadium's foundations to its outward completion. The scene reminded me in miniature of a television programme I had lately watched about the Great African Rift. Hence the title of the first sonnet in this sequence:

NUMBER ONE
A Sonnet Sequence

75. THE GREAT WIMBLEDON RIFT

Famed Wimbledon, the tennis Koh-i-Noor,
The aspirant's star sceptre, diadem
Of dreams, creates new amphitheatre gem,
Fine set for knights to tilt in joust as yore.

The brazen vintage year of ninety-five
Sees Ra the searing sun-god flay the earth
To strip the flesh from soil and supine rock
With molten fire, in cataclysmic shock,
The waters of a giant stadium's birth,
Designed to clasp an em'rald in its gyve …

This latest progeny a signal son,
Endowed with ev'ry part the gods could give
To serve its acolytes and so to live,
Henceforward always known as Number One.

Next the vast brontosaurus-necked cranes that swivelled to find their bombing mark. Sometimes they seemed to be swinging into my windows – almost within touching range:

76. THE CRANES

With supple majesty the titan cranes
Advance, retreat and pause in minuet;
Gyrate again, once more to skirmish; yet
Well fixed within their sky-high arcs and planes,
They never breach the tenets of their craft
But raise or lower loads with fluent ease,
Responding with precision to decrees
Of pilot hands, and effortlessly waft
Prodigious weights across the empty sky:
Thence, steered by signs from wheedling red-back ants,
Each scrupulously drops its freight and plants
Another prop; then hies away once more to ply.

These courteous cranes do overlord the scene;
They swing to conquer, never to demean.

Below, the diggers ('grabs', as I thought of them) zigzagged too and fro, endlessly active – digging, being filled, accepting craneloads, transporting, replacing – all in the style of circus performers displaying their skills:

77. THE GRABS

Below obsequious genuflecting grabs
Do grovel, scrape and, servile to their lords,
Play busybody parts with urgent greed.
Their jaws, like claws of elongated crabs,
Attack the soil within the shoring boards;
They scour and scoop, then spin to answer need
And fill a lorry-load or hole in ground:
They knead and smooth, solidifying space,
Manoeuvring with a sinuous sly squirm:
Their animated glee as if they clowned,
And playful gesture might e'en yet misplace
But 'tis the driver's will that doth affirm.

These digger denizens that roam The Rift
Incessantly maraud to shift and lift.

After this I'd exhausted my inspiration and spirit as what threatened to be total financial ruin loomed, for I was a Lloyds 'Name'. However, by a miracle it was averted. Thereafter I sought the sun in France, where I alternated with Guernsey and, of course, Wimbledon for the weeks surrounding the Championships.

Pat and I first discovered Saint Raphaël in the autumn of 1997. It is a comparatively small seaside town on the Côte d'Azur. It is hospitable, the people friendly and proud, a pride that perhaps is inbred, for many of them are descended from Roman Empire families.

The Hotel Continental on the Esplanade is as friendly under its owner, Lucien Wagner, as is La Collinette in Guernsey under Andrew Chambers and his mother, Peggy. I find I am able to work at both hotels. France offers the added pleasure of a wide countryside to forage in for places and things of interest.

The year 1997 was when I met a wonderful couple spending a week's holiday in Guernsey. Their table at La Collinette was next to mine, so I got to know Sir John and Lady Bailey, John and Marion. He is the Procurator General (Head of the Government's Legal Service). His name first gave me the idea, though clearly he does not try criminal cases. Marion says I have hit him off exactly:

78. OLD BAILEY

Old Bailey is full fearsome decked
At first sight;
But then, despite,
Shows different view that does reflect
True judgment's light.

Stern law does opt to reconcile
A kinder mien
That loosens lien
With courtroom quip and judge's wile
To soften scene.

Wisdom is poised to balance truth;
Compassion's ray
Doth brighten day;
The arbiter drains cup of ruth
For final say.

30 December 1997

It has been during our autumn and spring visits to St Raphaël since 1997 that nearly all the remaining verses in this book have been written. Meanwhile, Pat has started her own form of pointillisme in some most attractive small pictures.

This was largely forced on her by there being no space for an easel in her room. These vignette still lives are a considerable contrast to her natural bold style.

Staying on the seafront as we were and – in my own case – wanting to walk along the flat, it was the natural pitch for our routine exercise. It was fascinating to watch the Sunday strollers:

SUNDAY AT ST RAPHAËL
A Sonnet Sequence

79. BESIDE THE SEA

The traffic forges on the sea-front road.
The sunshine sparks the bay and esplanade
'Twixt sea-wall set with Greek key-fret inlaid
And pollard planes or palms dressed à la mode.

In quick-spot peck prospecting seedy spoil,
The pigeons quest and quirk round yachtsmen's toes:
A school-walk gaggle giggles as it goes;
The master leads, the mistress rallies toil.

All ages pass, parading sea-scape stage,
The seniors slow of foot, youth's joyous stride
Unheeding thrall of precious time to bide,
Their elders seeking solace on each page.

As butterflies are born to preen and die,
The wavelets' ripples breathe their death-kiss sigh.

Mind you, you have to keep a wary lookout for roller-skaters, skateboarders, cyclists – even motor-cyclists (quite illegally of course) who would all consider this to be their natural domain. I always walk like a Johnny Head-Down, which was just as well. I was less likely to be caught underfoot by dogs' droppings:

80. TURD WORLD

High-stepping poodles, Fifi and Froufrou,
Indulgently loose-leashed by doting dame,
Do pause to stake aristocratic claim
With individual pee-pee or poo-poo.

Then, after connoisseur's judicious sniff,
Each leaves pure paradigm, rich Saveloy,
Bon viveur off'rings others may enjoy,
The knowing nostril relishing the whiff.

Such pungency! Oh, exquisite delight!
What subtle variations on the theme
Combine for canine taste's ecstatic dream,
Exploding bursts of Borealis light!

Fifi and Froufrou, noses in the air,
Do proudly prance, a pair without compare.

POOPS !

"KA -BOOM !!"

Every few weeks, Sunday is enlivened by a parade, celebrating some calendar event. A popular one is Mimosa Day, signifying the short season of this tree with its beautiful yellow flowers.

On these occasions, a parade tribune stands in front of the hotel and barriers to the motorcade route are put up, so that the procession of colourful floats can be well viewed and the town's officials can show their support. A band plays and their tuning up in readiness is deafening to sensitive ears:

81. TRIBUNE TUNE-UP

The pollard planes stand firm, each pristine lopped,
Presenting slap-drilled arms to heavens high,
Like artichokes re-rooted to the sky,
A guardsmen's honour troop, heads standard cropped.

The coloured drums reverberate around
In cruel cacophony at hearing's cost,
The mind is deadened, inner sight is lost,
All blurs in blunting bursts of brutal sound.

The crowd-controlling fences are ranged out,
The tribunes escalate in jury rig.
The drummers ready for their joyful jig,
Impromptu band to beat the rhythm shout.

All is now set to signal start's go-go
For typic Riviera Sunday show.

Like many men, or other shopping appendages to a busy housewife acquiring her week's household supplies in a supermarket, I have done my time with a trolley overflowing with goodies:

82. AISLES OF THE BLEST

Give me the trolley, Dolly,
And I'll wander the aisles with you,
Your faithful attendant, Dolly,
Piling folly on folly,
As we sift the bargains through.

Fifty per-cent off dried prunes –
Or here's something that's better still –
End of the line savoury scoones
Gift-wrapped with give-away spoons,
And cream that's over the hill?

*As we all know, some of these choice offers
are unpopular or dicy items being got rid of
as fast as possible and some are genuine
bargains to entice us into a buying frenzy.*

I know I may be blind or hopelessly biased, but I have never been able to understand why lines of prose, however figurative, imaginative and well-written (unless in blank-verse rhythm), with no attempt at rhyme should be sanctified as poetry: nor why the ghastly objects and sights presented as art (under the guise of being Modern) these days should be so admired: and particularly why such rubbish can command huge prices in some strange form of inverted snobbery.

What really made me start coming round to the view that the world is going downhill fast, captured by a new and virulent form of contemporary madness, was the sale by one of the two big auction houses a couple of years or so ago of a modern kitchen chest (admittedly beautifully made) for £65,000. Since then there have been many even more extreme examples of the 'art' of Damian Hirst and his acolytes fetching huge sums. At least the chest can be used – even if the word 'art' is abused:

83. THE PSEUDOCRAT

Why this viral thirst
For the very worst
Of those works accursed
By Damian Hirst?

They may be well tooled
But don't be fooled.

It is not art.
It's just a fart
In our faces –
Some might say faeces.

There is another view to be held. The art world is sane and I – and many others, I'm sure – have lost my reason. Then there was the huge expenditure undertaken to mark the Millennium with the Greenwich Dome – a ripple on the keys by improviser Mandelson:

84. PIPE DREAM
(With apologies to Samuel Taylor Coleridge)

In Greenwich town did Mandelson
A state-staked leisure dome decree,
Where Thames the spendthrift river ran
Through gold vaults measureless to man,
Draining the Treasury.

I've always enjoyed limericks and trying to write them. They are tricky creatures, not so easily tamed. It was whilst staying at La Collinette in Guernsey last autumn and over Christmas that I became aware, through my mentor, Ken Fletcher, of the Guernsey Millennium Eisteddfod. Entry time was near, with various poetic headings one could compete in, including limericks.

My enthusiasm produced the following, several inspired by an article, or even a snippet, in The Daily Telegraph:

85. ON THE RIGHT TACK

An athlete who hailed from Kampala
Trained on chicken tikka masala.
    He found when in need
    It gave him the speed
Of native fleet-footed impala.

86. DRAMBUSTER

A muggins on tour of Madeira
Decided its wines were supeira
    To call of any port –
    At least, so he thought
Till his thick head became somewhat cleira.

That was entirely spawned by inspiration, including the heading.
Getting an appealing title is so important but can be oh, so difficult!
I was pleased with:

87. NO MATTER

An inexperienced traveller in space
Met a meteor, alas face to face.
   At a speed near light
   It was worse than a plight –
The result: he dissolved without trace.

But I nearly fell off my chair as I was checking on 'Rumbustious' for the next when by chance I hit on the perfect:

88. RAMBUNCTIOUS

A randy Manx ram called Lancelot
Was often given to prance-a-lot:
    When tupping his ewes,
    He would so enthuse
That they soon conjoined to dance-a-lot.

A word I did not know – rambunctious – but spot on for meaning horny play.

There followed two glorious stories highlighted in The Daily Telegraph, *one about an 82 year-old who had acquired some medical prescription forms and with aplomb made some out to himself for Viagra. To me it seemed natural that he should come from Niagara, which proved to be his downfall:*

89. SELF-HELP

An impatient old man of Niagara
Once prescribed for himself some Viagra.
   His nickname was 'Red' –
   Quite blushing in bed –
Till he felt the full force of high 'agua'.

His fatal suspense in love's thrall
Took him over the lip of the fall
   For what proved eternity
   He pulsed with paternity
And experienced a thrill without pall.

But the story that went straight to the heart (front-page stuff) was that of a solitary Galapagos tortoise who was:

90. THE LAST OF THE LINE

A tortoise called George from Galapagos,
With face like a head of asparagus,
    Was the last of his line,
    So did nothing but pine
For a mate or something analagous.

So extreme was the shellback's sad plight
That some scientists took up his fight.
    'We know a good way –
    We'll use DNA –
So roll over, young fella, hold tight.'

Their research soon revealed a near strain,
That gave George life and hope to attain.
    They brought up girl cousins
    In cohorts of dozens
To let George try again and again.

Alas, still there's no news to relate,
As to whether he's serviced a mate.
 So we may never know
 If Virgo intacto
Has been able to overcome fate.

I felt I'd done George proud and so it seemed did the Eisteddfod judges, who gave me the gold 'Honours Certificate' for the limerick category. I was astonished and very proud.

By now – with the advent of the Millennium – I knew I should publish this book, so I got busy writing. The following all came in response to this urge between November 1999 and March this year – most of them completed in St Raphaël.

The first was 'In the Dark?', an experience I witnessed in early January while having my hotel breakfast at Orange in the Rhône Valley. A man was threading his way though the empty tables and chairs:

91. IN THE DARK?

I saw a blind man walking,
His stick it seemed was stalking,
Acting as guide.
Unerring, dodging baulking,
As if a friend were talking
Just by his side.

None dared to show him pity –
Of all souls in the city
So well contained.
But no-one sang a ditty,
Nor larked one little bitty.
They all refrained.

His stick could clear his progress,
But time was now the ogress,
Or so it seemed.
His wrist-watch fingered – oh yes!
He wasn't late, so no stress –
Just as he'd deemed.

His temp'rament could savour
Experience with full flavour
That fate allowed.
From die he'd never quaver,
Nor seek a special waiver,
This man unbowed.

Though blind he had the aura
Of one who sees much surer
Both time and tide.
He'd never be a borer,
Nor clever, witty scorer
Off someone's pride.

As years tolled he'd grow older,
A presence at his shoulder,
Assurance shield.
His mind would never moulder,
Musings would always smoulder;
He'd never yield.

He was incredible and made me feel proud of the human race. It's a race that is daily changing its character and aims.

But some things are eternal, one being 'Boy Meets Girl'. The conventions – or nowadays lack of them – vary. As ever, an opportunist steps in:

"HELLO!"

92. BOY MEETS GIRL

They say there's always been an interplay
That sparks between two folk at their first meeting;
And makes the next an easier glad greeting,
Or grates and gears instinctive disarray.

Now US science seeks avoid dismay
By electronic button for hearts bleating
Forlorn ... forsaken ... stood-up ... eyes entreating –
With Friend Link's artificial love display.

A flash! Now shed your shackle shyness. Nerve –
And be – yourself, for best-of-all impression.
Do that and each sustained sequential session
May find you thought love's dream without reserve.

So press your button. Linking is the tie
That may lend love and leave no need to sigh.

There can't be a TV viewer who hasn't groaned when seeing yet another tour de farce of handshaking outside No 10 Downing Street, or similar camera shot venues – handshakes of accord. This is going to be all right, chaps. Or is it?

93. GLAD HAND

What does a handshake mean today?
A camera shot at hack's command
To demonstrate sincerity
Of cocktail sealing pact with prey?
Or no, 'Well, folks, I'll be godarned!
It's Al with new dexterity.'

'Al who? Oh Him! Dear old Al Gore?
You mean to say he's in the news
And heading for the Demo Vote?
Well, he knows how to shake a paw
And give "impromptu" interviews,
Inane but crafted for a quote.'

Or Blair or Kohl and Clinton, too,
Give abject lessons in lesioned truth.
They are agreed, so pump the handle
To show accord and mirage view.
'One more? Okay, my friends, but strewth,
I'll now make way for son of Mandel!'

From shallow ends to deeper waters.
The hand may hide a blade or gun,
Enforcing black heart's wicked will.
It's not the trust grandparents taught us,
Staking good faith in deal just done,
Not making work for burdened Bill.

St Raphaël
30 February 2000

It was in January that I felt impelled to try to evoke the Cresta Run for both expert, which Loon (Alasdair Hilleary) my illustrator is, and the novice which, in 1948 at the Winter Olympics, I was. I felt I especially wanted to for Loon's sake, and only hoped I could accomplish what is not an easy task to bring alive in words, let alone rhyming pentameter verse:

94. CRESTA RETROSPECT

Sole BBC OB events reporter
In Moritz '48, I was cavorter
On carefree round of piste, bob-run and ice-rink,
Relaying stories of each cliff-hang spice kink;
But always coming back to quizz the Cresta,
The demonstration sport, the terror tester
Of courage, nerve and skill, allied to ply
With sense and soul's internal sceptic eye.

Inevitably I was drawn to 'Top',
Whence riders flung themselves in diving drop
Down what appeared near precipice of slope,
With no sustaining glimpse for hero's hope
That there could be a shadow of solution
Before disintegrating dissolution.

The rider, plus fours, woollen jersey clad,
With toe-spiked boot, both knee and elbow pad
Of leather, eyes be-goggled, hard crash helmet
To shield his head – as if an armoured pelmet,
Awaits the signal for his dice and dare,
His misty breath near freezing on the air.
The Cresta course is best run early morn
E'er sun so hot that track is shred and torn.

He stands at 'Lists' like knight of old for joust,
His steed a 'skeleton'. He's not long roust
From sleep. At clash of 'Charge', be he unsaddled,
He'll find no quarter when by trammels straddled.
The gleaming sword hangs sinister in front,
With curling scabbard causing many a shunt.

The bell rings. Rider comes to fore, then gives
Two ... three ... four timing swings while still he lives ...
Takes running dive from 'Top', before man-hurling
Self face-down, pressed flat, skeleton then swirling
Round contours of sheer ice, the sheath of blade,
Rebuilt each year and always sinuous made;

A vicious Dervish-brandished cruel kris twirling
Agleam, accelerating (the steel sterling)
Toward eventual swift decapitation –
No time to feel blind terror's palpitation:

Each nerve is strung to twang at teeter-tilt,
The rider hurtling, after-burn at hilt;
Mercurial plummet like antique child's puzzle,
The silver ball sure-steered with scarce a nuzzle
Of crested cliffs – each touch adds tenths of second
To sum of final time by stop-watch reckoned.

I watched these gladiators deftly guiding,
And saw how body sway left banks eliding,
Till 'Finish' rise restrained the onward rush,
Eased rider's riven breath, restored a hush
For final focus of intent attention
To Cresta time, in hope of honour mention ...

*Just one word of explanation now. The novice goes from 'Junction'
only – that's two-fifths of the way down the course. He doesn't have
that terrifying drop from 'Top':*

The normal novice, well-keeled volunteer,
Who knew his great ability to steer
A Jaguar or Alfa Romeo
And hold his course quite sure but never slow,
Might step to start, eager to have a go.
Not so your dubious correspondent, who
Had seen too much and only too well knew
The risks attendant on the Cresta run
Ever to feel, 'It's just a bit of fun.'

But, come the final Sunday of The Games,
I suddenly perceived the subtle aims
Of experts like my mentor Jimmy Coats,
Himself past champion, now dispensing oats
Of vast experience. He had hooked my pride.
I owed it to him as my working guide,
And to the BBC to fly the flag.
If jibbing, I'd be just a Cresta slag.

And so I found myself, a lamb new-neutered,
Like squire transformed to knight and so accoutred,
Affecting unconcern with no brain function,
Aware of nothing save this ogre Junction,
Just wishing I'd the lever to switch line
And exit fast, uncaring of repine.

And now the bell, that dreaded death-throe blow,
And Jimmy's final caution, 'Take it slow ...
Seat slid back, so that spikes of runners bite ...
With toe-caps rake and rake ... You'll be all right ...
So stick to "brake and rake". Come safely down,
Getting the feel. No need to go to town.'

Now lying sprawled on skeleton askew,
My being blank, not knowing what to do,
A fish just landed, bound for monger's slab,
The gaff denied, no hope at which to grab;
Then suddenly, a push propels my start,
A prompting hand to help the weak at heart.

Oblivious thrall possesses as we slide,
The first bankina 'Rise', a right-hand ride
To aim for Battledore, a steeper right ...
All blotted out as runners take the bite

" RAKE!...RAKE!...**RAKE!**...**RAKE!**"

And slide becomes a glide. Spine-petrified,
Unnerved, I freeze ... I almost feel I've died ...
Until my haze is pierced by voice that cries,
'Ra...aaa...ke! ... Ra...a...ke! ... It's Jimmy halting my demise.

I've always had extremely fast reaction.
My feet plunge down. Immediate retraction ...
Has almost stopped the sled – alas, not quite.
In tenths the fateful slide anew begins
And swiftly gathers pace. My old jinx jinns
Have taken hold again. 'We're off!' they cry.
For them 'No reason why' – nor fear to die.

Explicit time and space possess no meaning,
One moment leftward, next to rightward leaning.
My 'ailerons' seem jammed. They are not working –
But not surprising. I'm disjointed, jerking
At pull and will of Cresta's grizzly grasp,
Just feeling each might be my life's last gasp.

Survival now is sum of all that matters,
The rest, it feels, already torn to tatters;
One moment breasting Shuttlecock's abyss,
The next in downward rush to 'Straight' for kiss
Of counter sides ... bash ... crash from one to t'other,
Quite impotent to steer the sled and smother
The force of impact ... Skeltering 'neath 'Bridge',
Till bruised and battered to a lump of squidge;

Cascading down this fear-inflecting funnel
Through monstrous typhoon-tightening wind tunnel,
Volcano spew side-slamming down to Scylla,
The siren rock ... aslew without a tiller
Or cox to steer around the vortex reach
Of 'Whirlpool' banking, the Charybdis leech.

The sled is gathering pace on downward dip
To 'Leap' (my nerves still screaming 'Please don't flip!'),
Misnomer though at speed of first attempt ...
And so to 'Rise' and finish most unkempt,
Too slow to reach the top, reversing slip
To flop inglorious, then abandon ship ...
Sides heaving, gulping air, alive if stranded ...
At least I'm still aboard and now safe landed.

The PA hiccups curtly to announce
'Time ninety four' ... though giving every ounce!
Just twice the record. Maybe not so bad,
Better than Flynn – two minutes Errol had!
By now my being so completely shriven,
I feel my Cresta fears have been forgiven.

It was with trepidation that I awaited Loon's verdict on his return from his annual Cresta outing. 'By the way, I liked your Cresta piece,' he said laconically. What relief!

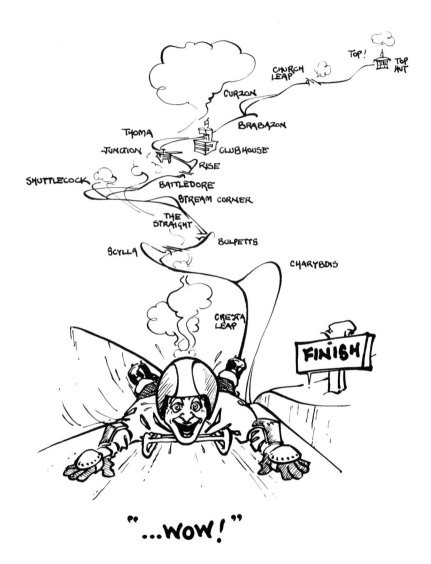

Now I propose to go further back in time – at least to start with – to my Papuan jungle experience and my first encounter with:

95. BLOOD LUST

When I was young and venturing
Into true life (or so I thought),
With will to be apprentice writer,
I had as my indenturing
The straits and stress so stretched and straught
Felt by a tropic jungle fighter.

New Guinea beckoned – so romantic,
With gold pay dirt below the mud.
'Twas there I met with glutton leeching,
Each piteous trunk in spasm frantic
To stretch on scent of any blood,
Beseeching, at the double reaching.

With crack troops circling, infiltrating,
Pervading every inch of trail,
My squelching boots could bypass not:
The smell of blood was so elating
They sped in sprint of fierce assail
To cling and suck and form gorged clot.

Once on, they'd thread through any hole
Around the tongue or eye for lace.
They'd never let themselves be thwarted,
Just sought the breach to storm their goal.
If boot too strong they'd climb its face,
So mission's fill be not aborted.

Not likely! Each would wend a way.
However taut your pant or puttee,
They'd pick-hold traverse crease thigh-high,
Unless suppressed by salt-bomb stay,
Or fag's fire-tip as make-shift suttee.
'Don't pull to sever. Never try.'

Just heat or salt will zap the nerve
And break the hold of suckered grip –
Blood-glutted body drops as spoor;
But pull and that will only serve
To leave the sucker's sickly clip,
So starting suppurating sore.

" YUM YUM! HERE COMES FRESH BLOOD! "

In time parenthesis it's weird
That men were trained to be a 'leech',
The name the doctors were then called.
For leeching blood some tumours queered,
Or might a fever's crimson bleach –
And so, 'twas hoped, the sickness stalled.

Today we have new breeds of leeches,
Prospecting pay dirt sensed on hand.
They scent our blood, they scent our money
In pension schemes, on foreign beaches,
Wherever lily-gilding's planned
To lure to lotus land of honey.

By TV ad for star-struck souls,
Or callous use of pet appeal,
As sympathetic mortgage lenders,
They wheedle wealth from spellbound proles,
Not always bothered to conceal
Contempt for us when hooked as spenders.

These modern leeches seldom heal
The hearts and hopes they've often broken
By gold allure of gambled gain;
Inured to torment victims feel,
A bankrupt's dividend their token
Return for all the untold pain.

But Nemesis nears those who've preyed
To guillotine such gangrened guilt,
It's salt-bomb ticking retribution;
Whether by seizure or bare blade,
Its vengeance fire-tipped to the hilt,
The lightning strike, no attribution.

To those in desperation drowning
Swift guardian wings arrive in time,
Their piteous protégés to prise
From devils' hold, their rescue crowning
With silent sympathy sublime
And exhortation, 'Come, arise!'

St Raphaël
20-27 January 2000

Have I contrived too happy an ending? Some people are lucky and I have a firm belief in guardian angels. Mine has often saved me but, alas! not from indiscretion, one of my worst sins and for that I have suffered – quite justly of course.

The last poem I intended to write for this book, at St Raphaël in Millennium March of time, relies on an accident of history, which could so easily have occurred. What fun I thought to have a 'supposing' with its consequences in:

96. EVOLUTION PERADVENTURE

As well as plants, potato and tobacco,
If only Raleigh's gaze had lit – alack, oh! –
On prickly Chilean Brobdingnag pipe-cleaner,
The evergreen that might have changed demeanour
Of mediaeval evolution thinking ...
For then there could have been a lemur-linking
By Newton who was pondering a story
Discovered in some papers to the glory
Of great globe-gleaner, questing Marco Polo,
Who made historic journey (but not solo –
Papa and uncle with him) to the court
Of Kublai Khan, whose empire lay athwart
The frontiers of far-flung eastern races.

Like Grandad Genghis, Kublai held the traces
Of Mongol might's dominion ... Marco wrote
This – more beside ... one fascinating note,
Deciphered by Erasmus, first related
A Chinese legend, told in whispers bated,
Of Big Foot yeti, simian-shaped wild man,
Deduced by tracks high on mountain span,
And whistling signal of his bound'ry beat,
Prescribed with stools undreamt as human feat.
'Twas also said that Big Foot was descended
From 'Little Mouse', a minute monkey, ended
In ancient cataclysmic supervention;
Just myth – no scientific apprehension.

The sage, now standing under furry fuzzle
And feeling lowest branch give spiky nuzzle,
Alerting his prophetic sharp perception
Of early man's original conception,
Clapped hand to fertile cranium's cliff-face brow,
Exclaiming, 'Gadzooks! I've resolved it now.
We all, from king to squire to humble flunkey
Are primate issue from the proto-monkey.
Then, turning to the spur of clarity,
Pronounced his debt with measured gravity,
'O pricking Muse, I name thee monkey-puzzle!
May never time suppress your bite with muzzle ...'

This left young Darwin little else to do,
Save shift discerning gaze to look anew;
Then, punning 'The Descent Of Man', to trace
The modern Gadarenes in downhill race
To prime-so-evil vicious degradation –
The Devil pressing greed's acceleration
To Man's dire downfall, dreaded extirpation.

16 March 2000
St Raphaël

(Inspired by an item in The Daily Telegraph.*)*

*But another 'supposing' appealed. This would be a piece of future
history, I hoped.:*

97. APOTHEOSIS OF A BATSMAN

Mike Atherton, with Mr Standfast stare,
And elbow shield to blunt fast bowlers' ire,
With fierce resolve, frustrating fury fire
Of biggest guns the enemy might bear.

His shoulder points with steady two-eyed aim,
His radar judgment measures ball's spear line;
Imperfect length he metes with crack condign.
His stubborn stance defiance doth proclaim.

His 'squared-up' vice now chained by tutored feet,
His sights fine-set on salving honour's grail,
Defence alert against surprise assail –
A cent'ry would be very sweet and meet,

Just right in England's Oval climax need.
'Time' has been called for such a special deed.

Acknowledged by all lovers of true judgment, impartial but spiced with wicked wit, was the famous Daily Telegraph *cricket writer E W Swanton. His report of such an Atherton innings would have acclaimed the feat with lofty historic comparison and pithy contemporary metaphor. He was still working when he made the Millennium at a robust 92. Then, a few days into the new year, he found the umpire's finger raised. I'd always admired him. His instinctive batting stroke was forward, so this was my tribute:*

98. DOWN THE LINE

So it's goodbye to Swanton,
To most of us just Jim.
His words were never wanton –
They were, straight bat, just him.

But it was not the last. As dot.com shares boomed on every stock exchange, I could not help feeling that somewhere the Devil had a hand in it. The world's madness seemed suddenly to have rocketed into accelerating expansion, pacing the Universe. In what follows I'm sure I show myself to be the bigoted ignoramus that I am:

99. BEDLAM.COM

Wherever you go, the mobile phone
Will soon encroach on comfort's zone,
P'raps dining somewhere at your ease,
Or anywhere that you should please,
Some mobile rings to draw attention,
But often only stirs dissension.

Dictators stride, with ear to phone,
Ignoring that they're not alone.
Important calls they are at sight,
But importuning us with blight,
Oblivious of all sound they air,
Of those nearby quite unaware.

The mobile phone, today's necessity
Is conduct's gross overt obsessity.
Wher'eer you walk the buzzing bees
Are sucking sound from stamen's tease.
They're now allied to website tangle
In evolution's new-found wangle.

Do we subscribe to world-wide bomb
Of madhouse bedlam's mark dot com?
Shall we be caught up in the Web
And see our privacy fast ebb?
Then have our mind's device well milked,
So fortune's prize we find is bilked?

How long before we see our revels
Prorogued by Opposition devils?
How long before we are Web-netted,
With no escape, just internetted?
We must abstain, avoiding panic
To shrive ourselves from Site Satanic.

*I see I'm not totally unsupported. Recently the Archbishop of York
expressed his concern at some of the ramifications of the Internet. Oh
well ... I wonder whether another mode will ever come into being,
such as SPOT ON for instance? Dot.com is so boring, it's like
applause that has got into a repeating groove.*

To end, I'm determined not to be so serious. The following event occurred in 1948 and is part of what I've so far written of Wimbledon – The Age of the Icons *as a sequel to* The Ballad of Worple Road. *I've only got to 1955. I hope it will see the light of day.*

100. HIGH JINKS

Next came a year of sunshine, each day fine,
A year when history was made by pine
Marten – as Yanks would say, to us a grey
Squirrel – which seized its chance to brighten play.
Blond Dutchman, Hans Van Swol, in tilting sway
Of battle versus French Abdessalam
Was fading in the fifth, 3–5. Alarm
Bells ringing, when the cheeky little chappie
Chose Centre stage to show how very happy
He was performing 'fore such ardent audience.
So, jinking to warm music of encorediants,
He blithely swerved from clutching hands of linesmen
Who clearly joined him in the fun, just pinesmen
Playing his game. He'd show them! Laughter grew
As, twisting like a Guscott, he dodged through ...
Till now no longer game ... But cry and hue ...
In fact becoming an official stew! ...

The game's famed stage now in the pert possession
Of squirrel clown? Impertinent ingression! ...
Such breach of rules should suffer swift repression ...
The problem though, how to enforce expression? ...
The red-faced linesmen welcomed new recruit
In shape of ball-boy taking up pursuit.
The squirrel now cavorted even better,
As if the chase had loosened every fetter.

He flirted closer still in freedom's joy.
When sudden seized, he promptly bit the boy,
Believing justified recrimination
For halting *his* game, causing 'foul' frustration.
While swift removed, he still had much to say.
His 'nutty' fans just cheered him all the way ...
Van Swol admired this virtuosity
From racket perch. Now bellicosity
Was brimming after minutes three of rest.
He won 13–11, still full of zest,
Then raised his eyes in thanks to girdered nest,
Returned next year, the grey one on his vest.

Thank you for being with me. See you next time, as they all say now,
for life is perilously fraught with goodbyes.

But wait! ... Something's gnawing at my mind ... Ah yes! ... A little matter of 'Chalk or Cheese':

101. CHALK OR CHEESE

The limpet, or patella so vulgata,
Provides us with astonishing new data.
Its busy jaws are surely undermining
Those white cliffs, which were England's breastplate lining
Against the tyrant Hitler, who was trying
To conquer us; thereby the upstart vying
With William. Fortune, at our side rebating
Defence, gave pause. Aware of underrating,
He turned, fought Russian winter's power corrosion,
Bear-hugged to face fate's second front implosion.

A thousand years' Teutonic rule he boded.
For aeons maybe, those cliffs have been eroded
By munching jaws of closely clinging limpet
That undercuts – its motto, 'Never skimp it'.
The difference of cheese from chalk, so puzzling
For some, has not a qualm for limpet guzzling:
The greedy gastropod, gourmet gastronome
Long wot the secrets of fleshed echo-pome,
Its food cliff algae – with fine chalk ingestion
That guarantees it such superb digestion.

Now for millennium crunch or stiff cliff-facer,
Which, come to think on it, is quite a bracer.
If limpet life is cushy, independent,
Its star of algae sign in the ascendant,
Perhaps we should beware grey mollusc matter,
Not think ourselves superior and so flatter
Our egos? They've good formulae for living,
How long? There lies the nub of my misgiving.
Have they time past deciphered gene formation?
Do they control the levers of life's station?
Could we be shunted from our ortho-carway
To buffer bonfire of an auto-da-fe?

" MMMM....I COULD MURDER A WHITE CLIFF! "